240 Writing Topics with Sample Essays Q211-240

LIKE TEST PREP

Copyright © 2014 LIKE TEST PREP

All rights reserved.

ISBN: **1499619553**
ISBN-13: **978-1499619553**

DEDICATION

To the LIKE Family

Disclaimer: The opinions expressed herein are those of the author and not of the publisher, LIKE TEST PREP.

Contents

How to Write an Essay..vi

Q211. Some parents give their children money on a monthly basis. At what age should children receive an allowance and how much should they receive?...................2

Q212. Who do you like the better, athletes or entertainers?...4

Q213. Describe your most unforgettable day. Why will you never forget this day?...........6

Q214. Who will you remember the most after you finish school, your friends or your teachers?...8

Q215. Describe your idea of a happy life..10

Q216. Which genre of books do you enjoy reading the most? Why?...............................12

Q217. Which fruit do you like the most? Why?..14

Q218. What is your favorite TV show and why?..16

Q219. What is your favorite movie and why?..18

Q220. Compare the advantages and the disadvantages of Smart Phones.......................20

Q221. Which option is healthier, eating three large meals a day or eating four to five small meals a day?...22

Q222. If you could win a lot of money, how much would you win and why?...................24

Q223. We are continuously learning and doing new things in life and often times we fail at our first attempt. Describe your first attempt to gain something new...................26

Q224. Describe your ideal holiday resort...28

Q225. What is your biggest ambition in life?...30

Q226. Which family member has influenced you the most? Why is this person a positive or negative role model in your life?..32

Q227. Where do you see yourself in twenty years?..34

Q228. What quality or qualities do you look for in a best friend?..................................36

Q229. Parents should be required to pay for their children's university education. Do you agree or disagree with this statement?...38

Q230. Describe the qualities of a good citizen?...40

Q231. What are the most important qualities of a good teacher?.................................42

Q232. What qualities does a good student have to have?..44

Q233. What would you change about your country opportunity?.................................46

Q234. Do you agree or disagree with the following statement? An eye for an eye. Why or why not?...48

Q235. What is the most important job or task you have ever had? Why was it important?...50

Q236. What are the advantages and disadvantages of studying abroad?......................52

Q237. Describe your dream job. Why is it your dream job?..54

Q238. At what age is it appropriate to allow a child to stay at home alone?...................56

Q239. Some people say that the quality of a product is more important. Others say that the price of a product is more important. Which statement do you agree with and why?...58

Q240. How will you help a foreigner learn about your country?...................................60

How to Write an Essay: Outline

Outline your argument and ideas in the following way so that you can easily form an introduction paragraph. In order to write an essay in 25-30 minutes, you should train yourself so that you can finish your outlines in 5-10 minutes. Here is how to do so.

Prompt (question): "If you have an opportunity to send your child to study abroad, would you have him/her educated in the US or in your home country?"

1. Argument: I will have my child educated in the United States.
2. Support 1: My child can learn English better.
3. Support 2: My child can experience various languages and cultures.
4. Support 3: My child can play sports.
5. Thesis: Since my child can be better educated in the United States, I will send him/her to study in the United States. (argument+why)

1. Argument: State your argument clearly.
2. Support 1: Give specific reasons and examples.
3. Support 2: Give specific reasons and examples.
4. Support 3: Give specific reasons and examples.

   Good writers do not give similar reasons to support their argument. In other words, their three reasons (supports) should be distinguishable from each other.

5. Thesis: Usually a thesis appears in the middle or at the end of the introduction. It has to contain the rephrased main argument (should not be the same as the main argument) + why.

How to Write an Essay 1: Essay Types

In general, there are four types of argumentative (persuasive) essays.

1) experience & example
2) prefer
3) agree/disagree
4) compare and contrast or advantages and disadvantages

With the first three essays, it is easier to write a five paragraph essay.

5 paragraph essay (experience & example, prefer, agree/disagree)
Intro – The paragraph should be at least 3-5 sentences.
Support 1 - The paragraph should be at least 3-5 sentences.
Support 2 - The paragraph should be at least 3-5 sentences.
Support 3 - The paragraph should be at least 3-5 sentences.
Conclusion-The paragraph should be at least 3-5 sentences.

Sometimes it is easier to write a four paragraph essay.

4 paragraph essay (compare and contrast, advantages and disadvantages)
Intro – The paragraph should be at least 3-5 sentences.
Advantages-The paragraph should be at least 3-5 sentences.
Disadvantages-The paragraph should be at least 3-5 sentences.
Conclusion-The paragraph should be at least 3-5 sentences.

How to Write an Essay 2: Introduction

Your outline should easily become your introduction without useless words.

1. Argument: I will have my child educated in the US.
2. Support 1: My child can learn English better.
3. Support 2: My child can experience various languages and cultures.
4. Support 3: My child can play sports.
5. Thesis: Since my child can be better educated in the US, I will send him/her to study in the US. (argument+why)

Remember this? With the above, we can now easily create a complete introduction.

I will have my child educated in the US. <u>There are three reasons for this.</u> First, my child can learn English better. Second, my child can experience various languages and cultures. Third, my child can play sports. Because my child can be better educated in the US, I will send him/her to study in the US.

As you see, I only added one sentence to it. It is <u>underlined.</u> Isn't this simple?

How to Write an Essay 3: Body

All we have to do is to write the support and give specific reasons, details, and explanations.

For example,

①First of all, my child can learn English better in the US than in Korea. ② At school, my child will learn various subjects like Math, Science, Social Studies, Music, and Art in English. ③ Doing so, he/she can talk and write about various topics in English. ④ Then after school, my child will converse with others in English. ⑤his way, he/she will practice conversational English.

To explain, sentence ① is called the "topic sentence" and it contains the most important information. Sentences ②, ③, ④, and ⑤ contains specific examples and details that explain how the child will learn English better. After sentence ⑤, you can write a sentence about your next paragraph. However, this is not required.

Got it? You can write the other two supporting paragraphs the same way. Now, expand the second and the third paragraphs in your own words.

Second of all, my child can experience various languages and cultures in the US. (expand this like paragraph 2 and write at least four more sentences.)
Thirdly, my child can play various sports in the US (expand this like paragraph 2 and write at least four more sentences.).

How to Write an Essay 4: Conclusion

In the conclusion, you have to <u>rephrase</u>, <u>summarize</u>, and <u>conclude</u>. Here, you cannot simply copy the introduction. Instead, be creative.

①US education can benefit my child in many ways. ② My child can master the English language, broaden his horizons, and become more physically strong. ③ Therefore, if I have an opportunity to have my child educated in the US, I will not hesitate to send him abroad.

In sentence ①, I rephrased the <u>main argument</u>.

Introduction -> Conclusion
<u>main argument</u>: I will have my child educated in the US. -> US education can benefit my child in many ways.

In sentence ②, I summarized the <u>supports</u>.

<u>Supports</u>: My child can learn English better. My child can experience various languages and cultures. My child can play sports. -> My child can master English, broaden his horizons, and become more physically strong.

Point 3: I wrote the conclusion by rephrasing the <u>thesis</u>.

<u>Thesis</u>: As my child can be better educated in the US, I will send him/her to study in the US.-> If I have an opportunity to have my child educated in the US, I will not hesitate to send him abroad.

How to Write an Essay: Sample Essay

If I have the opportunity, I will have my child educated in the US. There are three reasons for this. First, my child can learn English better. Second, my child can experience various languages and cultures. Third, my child can play sports. Since my child can be better educated in the US, I will send him/her to study in the US.

First of all, my child can learn English better in the US than in Korea. At school, my child will learn various subjects like Math, Science, Social Studies, Music, and Art in English. Doing so, he/she can talk and write about various topics in English. Then after school, my child will converse with others in English. This way, he/she will practice conversational English.

Second of all, my child can experience various languages and cultures in the US. Unlike Korea, one can experience many different cultures and languages at a very close distance. For example, if my child wants to learn Vietnamese and their culture, he/she can go to the Vietnamese community and mingle there. If he/she wants to try the Italian cuisine, he/she can visit Little Italy. Moreover, there are many different ethnic festivals and ceremonies that my child can visit locally in the US.

Thirdly, my child can play various sports in the US. Unlike most Korean schools, US schools have excellent sports facilities. For example, many schools have swimming pools, football fields, basketball gym, tennis courts, and many others. Moreover, these schools encourage students to play sports. However, most Korean schools do not have such fine sports facilities and they discourage students from playing sports.

US education can benefit my child in many ways. My child can master English, broaden his horizons, and become more physically strong. Therefore, if I could have my child educated in the US, I will not hesitate to send him/her abroad.

Q211. Some parents give their children money on a monthly basis. At what age should children receive an allowance and how much should they receive?

A. Essay Outline

Argument: Children should be allowed to receive an allowance at age 10 and they should receive $30 a month.
Support 1: Children should start getting an allowance at 10 because they are too irresponsible before then.
Support 2: Thirty dollars is just enough to get odd things like school supplies or snacks.
Support 3: If you give a child more than $30 a month, they will not spend the money wisely. They will buy too much junk food.
Thesis: Because it is appropriate, children should be allowed to receive an allowance of thirty dollars at age 12.

B. Model Essay

When I was in elementary school, there were some kids in my class who received an allowance. I never got an allowance, even now as I start the 12th grade. However, I think that kids should receive an allowance and they should be able to start getting an allowance starting at age 12. However, it should not be for any more than $30 a month. This is because kids should learn how to be responsible with money; if a child receives any more money than this, he will not spend the money wisely.

First off, some children need to have an allowance in order to pay for things that the need when parents aren't around. For example, after school, some students go to academy in order to study more things in depth, including English, math, or even chemistry. Although there are a lot of kids going to academy earlier in life, there aren't many children going to academy for long hours before the age of 12. Therefore, it makes sense that 12-year-olds should get an allowance. These kids need to be able to buy dinner when their parents aren't there so they can concentrate on studying and preparing for tests.

Secondly, thirty dollars is just enough for a 12-year-old. There aren't many things that a child needs to buy. They don't have to pay for rent, groceries, gas, electricity, or even Internet access. Most of them just need a little bit of pocket money to spend after school occasionally. I think that 20 dollars is too low; they should get about a dollar a day in case they need to buy snacks or dinner or even some school supplies on their own. That way, just in case, they can buy a little something every day. I think that $30 is just enough for a 12-year-old.

Last, but not least, although parents could give more money than 30 dollars a month, they shouldn't. Children need to learn how to spend money wisely and how to be responsible. If parents give more than $30 a month, children almost certainly will spend the money on things they don't need like on a Wii. Back in middle school, almost all of the kids I knew who had an allowance of more than 30 dollars just spent the money on junk food. I'm sure that most of them ended up getting fat later in life, which could be prevented if they just didn't eat candy and cookies all the time. Some of the other kids I know with big allowances started buying and playing a lot of video games. As a result, they didn't study for many tests and they're now at the bottom of the class. Therefore, it is important not to give children too much allowance money.

All in all, there's a lot of good to come out of allowance. It makes parents' lives a lot more comfortable and it gives children a greater sense of independence. However, parents shouldn't start giving an allowance until their child is 12 and even then, they should only give the child $30 a month. That way, children will spend the money wisely and they will not become lazy or fat.

C. Useful Expressions

1. However, I think that kids should receive an allowance and they should be able to start getting an allowance starting at age 12.

2. First off, some children need to have an allowance in order to pay for things that they need when parents aren't around.

3. For example, after school, some students go to an academy in order to study more things in depth, including English, math, or even chemistry.

4. Therefore, it makes sense that 12-year-olds should get an allowance.

5. Most of them just need a little bit of pocket money to spend after school occasionally.

6. That way, just in case, they can buy a little something every day.

7. I think that thirty dollars is just enough for a 12-year-old.

8. If parents give more than thirty dollars a month, children almost certainly will spend the money on things they don't need like on a Wii.

9. I'm sure that most of them ended up getting fat later in life, which could be prevented if they just didn't eat candy and cookies all the time.

10. All in all, there's a lot of good to come out of allowance.

> **Q212. Who do you like the better, athletes or entertainers?**

A. Essay Outline

Argument: I prefer entertainers to athletes.
Support 1: Entertainers are creative, whereas athletes are not.
Support 2: I don't really like sports, so I don't much care for athletes.
Support 3: Entertainers give more money to charity than athletes.
Thesis: Because entertainers are so much better than athletes, I prefer entertainers to athletes.

B. Model Essay

Many people follow celebrity news in the media; it is all around us. Among the people we follow in the tabloids are entertainers and athletes. Entertainers, including singers, actors, and movie stars, are just some of the people I read about online or in magazines. However, I don't much care for the many athletes these magazines talk about, including figure skaters, runners, and soccer players. On the whole, I simply prefer entertainers to athletes.

First, I think that entertainers are more creative than athletes. Although both entertainers and athletes work hard, I don't think that athletes are generally creative in the sports arena. Playing soccer takes more skill than creativity; you need to be able to pass and shoot the ball in quick situations before being "creative." On the other hand, many entertainers have to be creative: for many of them, it is simply their job. For example, everyone thinks that Madonna is very creative: she reinvented the pop music genre by adding elements of other genres like electronica. When Madonna took a long hiatus between two of her albums, people thought that she was done with her career. Simply put, they thought her music was just too old to survive in a new generation. However, instead of pumping out the same music she had be doing for decades, she came back strong and released a very modern album. Madonna had to be very creative in order to create vastly different types of music herself.

Secondly, I don't much care for sports and as a result I don't much care for the people who play them. While some people are die hard about a particular sport or even some sports, I do not consider myself a sports fan. While I do enjoy watching some sports like tennis, I don't consider myself a fan at all. Because of that, I don't really follow up on how athletes do in their respective sports or know anything about their personal lives. However, I care a lot about music and movies. I go to the movie theater all the time and I always carry my headphones and mp3 player wherever I go. I read up on many of my favorite movie stars like Johnny Depp and Brad Pitt all the time and I watch movies with them every time I can. They just interest me more than athletes.

Last, I think that of the famous people who give to charity, the majority are people in the so-called entertainment industry. I've heard a lot, for example, about how George Lucas, the creator of the Star Wars franchise, has donated millions of dollars to his charity, the George Lucas Educational Foundation, to help students achieve their dreams. Additionally, actress Barbra Streisand has also donated a lot to her charity, the Barbra Streisand Foundation, in order to find cures for various diseases, including HIV/AIDS and breast cancer. However, I haven't heard about many athletes doing the same; I haven't heard about Michael Jordan donating any of his recent winnings to charity. Because entertainers seem more generous than athletes, I like entertainers more.

In conclusion, there are three reasons why I prefer entertainers to athletes. Entertainers are more creative and more generous than athletes and as a whole, I am apathetic when it comes to sports. Although I think athletes are important and we can read about them in the newspapers frequently, entertainers will always have a special place in my heart.

C. Useful Expressions

1. Many people follow celebrity news in the media; it is all around us.

2. Among the people we follow in the tabloids are entertainers and athletes.

3. However, I don't much care for the many athletes these magazines talk about, including figure skaters, runners, and soccer players.

4. On the other hand, many entertainers have to be creative: for many of them, it is simply their job.

5. When Madonna took a long hiatus between two of her albums, people thought that she was done with her career.

6. Simply put, they thought her music was just too old to survive in a new generation.

7. While some people are die hard about a particular sport or even some sports, I do not consider myself a sports fan.

8. While I do enjoy watching some sports like tennis, I don't consider myself a fan at all.

9. I read up on many of my favorite movie stars like Johnny Depp and Brad Pitt all the time and I watch movies with them every time I can.

10. Because entertainers seem more generous than athletes, I like entertainers more.

Q213. Describe your most unforgettable day. Why will you never forget this day?

A. Essay Outline

Argument: My most unforgettable day was my sixteenth birthday.
Support 1: All of my friends were there for my great birthday party.
Support 2: I got a lot of great gifts from my friends.
Support 3: When I drove the car, that night, I got into an accident.
Thesis: Because my sixteenth birthday was so bittersweet, it is a day I will never forget.

B. Model Essay

    My sixteenth birthday was both the best and the worst day of my life; it was such a mixture of both extreme happiness and intense sadness. In short, I had an amazing birthday party except right at the very end.

    First, my parents held me a great birthday party. All of my friends from school were at my birthday party. They put on their best clothes and we ended up having lots of fun. First, we went to a very fancy steakhouse. We ordered a lot of big steaks that were cooked just perfectly. There were also lots of good side dishes. I also remember having the best piece of cheesecake I ever had. Even though someone at another table complained that there was a fly in his soup, we didn't let that bother us. We kept laughing and giggling with our own conversation. After the restaurant, we went to a karaoke room. Even though I can't sing, my friends didn't say anything. We had lots of fun just trying to sing "Girls Just Wanna Have Fun."

    After we were done at the karaoke room, my parents took all of my friends and me back to our house to open my presents and have some more cake and coffee. I loved all of the gifts that I got from my friends: lots of clothes, perfume, lotions, and even a cute little bracelet that my friend Amber gave me. Some of the gifts were even quite expensive; one of my best friends, Tiffany, got me an mp3 player and my other best friend, Nicole, gave me a fur coat. However, they saved the best gift for last. When I was finished with my presents, I was a little sad. My father didn't give me a present and I was worried that he had procrastinated and couldn't get me a gift at the last minute, like he usually does. However, we heard a sound from outside. It sounded like an ice cream truck; my dad told me to go outside with him to investigate. As soon as I got outside, there was a car I didn't recognize in the driveway. It was brand new and my parents said that it was mine. I jumped up and down, screaming with excitement. I hugged and thanked my dad. It felt so great to have a new car.

    However, that's when the fun stopped and the misery began. I wanted to drive the car as soon as I saw it. I got my driver's license just that day, so I knew that I could drive the car confidently. I got into the car and started it up. I looked out my window and I moved my foot on the gas. As soon as I did, I realized I did something very, very wrong. I put the car in forward instead of in reverse. My friend was in front of the car and I hit her and the garage door. My beautiful new car now had a big dent in the front. I instantly started crying my eyes out. My car was gone and I was probably not going to get a new one for a while. My dad got angry at me for crashing the car and my mom tried to console me. I later found out that there was no insurance on the car, and so, my dad had to take out a loan to fix the damage to the house and the car. My friend, Kristen, though, had to go to the hospital. She recovered, but never talked to me again after that. I think that was the day I lost both my car and my friend.

To sum up, my birthday was the most unforgettable day in the world to me. I had so much fun until the moment I crashed the car and hurt my friend Kristen. Since then, I learned an important lesson: always double check you put the car in reverse when you're backing out of the driveway.

C. Useful Expressions

1. My sixteenth birthday was both the best and the worst day of my life.

2. Even though someone at another table complained that there was a fly in his soup, we didn't let that bother us.

3. Some of the gifts were even quite expensive.

4. However, they saved the best gift for last.

5. My father didn't give me a present and I was worried that he had procrastinated and couldn't get me a gift at the last minute, like he usually does.

6. It sounded like an ice cream truck; my dad told me to go outside with him to investigate.

7. However, that's when the fun stopped and the misery began.

8. I instantly started crying my eyes out.

9. I later found out that there was no insurance on the car, and so, my dad had to take out a loan to fix the damage to the house and the car.

10. I had so much fun until the moment I crashed the car and hurt my friend Kristen.

Q214. Who will you remember the most after you finish school, your friends or your teachers?

A. Essay Outline

Argument: I will remember my friends more than my teachers after I finish school.
Support 1: I will still hang out with my friends after I finish school.
Support 2: I spend more time talking to my friends compared to teachers.
Support 3: My friends support me all the time; my teachers have not done that.
Thesis: Because my friends mean so much to me, I will remember them more than teachers after I finish school.

B. Model Essay

    I have a lot of teachers in high school and they are all very great. Mr. Johnson is really funny, Mrs. Smith is really smart, and I learn a lot in Mr. Cooper's English class. However, if I had to pick which I would remember more about high school, my friends or my teachers, I would say my friends. This is because my friends and I hang out a lot after school, because I spend more time talking to my friends compared to my teachers, and because my friends support me 100%.

    To start off, I hang out with my friends a lot after schools. Sometimes we go to the movie theater and watch a movie or sometimes we go to the mall and buy some cute clothes. However, I can never do this with a teacher; my teachers are just too busy reading papers and grading my essays. My friends are always up for doing something, even if there is a quiz or test the next day. We just have so much fun talking, shopping, and laughing together. I will always remember that time and I hope that we continue to hang out after we finish high school.

    Secondly, I will remember my friends more than my teachers because I simply spend more time talking to my friends. Most of the time, when I talk to my teachers, it is because they want something for me or I want something for them. Just the other day, I tried to talk to Mr. Cooper. However, the only reason why I talked to him was because I was having trouble with my English class. We didn't really talk about anything except the class. Even though he told me I was still doing well, I didn't really get the chance to talk to Mr. Cooper about anything other than English, so I really don't know much about him other than his interest in English. However, I talk to my friends all the time, especially during lunchtime and we talk about everything and anything: boys, music, flowers, and even cake. I wish my teachers were more like my friends; if they were, I would remember them more.

    Thirdly, my friends always support me no matter what I do. If I am in a bad situation, my friends will always be there for me and never leave my side. For example, there was one time when I got into an accident. My friend, Caitlin who had just gotten a car, tried to start the car. She didn't really know how to drive and so when she meant to go backwards, she went forwards and hit me. I was in the hospital for a really long time. I never talked to Caitlin after that, but my other friends were nice enough to visit me in the hospital. One of them brought me soup and another one of my friends gave me a bouquet of flowers. My teachers, however, didn't come see me when I was in the hospital; they just gave my friend Tiffany all of this homework to give to me. It hurt to see them be so mean to me.

    In conclusion, I will absolutely remember my high school friends more than my high school teachers. We just do so many more things together and spend more time talking to them in and out of class. I hope that I keep in touch with my friends after we go our own ways in life.

C. Useful Expressions

1. However, if I had to pick which I would remember more about high school, my friends or my teachers, I would say my friends.

2. This is because my friends and I hang out a lot after school, because I spend more time talking to my friends compared to my teachers, and because my friends support me 100%.

3. However, I can never do this with a teacher; my teachers are just too busy reading papers and grading my essays.

4. My friends are always up for doing something, even if there is a quiz or test the next day.

5. Secondly, I will remember my friends more than my teachers because I simply spent more time talking to my friends.

6. However, I talk to my friends all the time, especially during lunchtime and we talk about everything and anything: boys, music, flowers, and even cake.

7. If I am in a bad situation, my friends will always be there for me and never leave my side.

8. One of them brought me soup and another one of my friends gave me a bouquet of flowers.

9. We just do so many more things together and spend more time talking to them in and out of class.

10. I hope that I keep in touch with my friends after we go our own ways in life.

Q215. Describe your idea of a happy life.

A. Essay Outline

Argument: My idea of a happy life involves three things: a good job, a happy family, and lots of money.
Support 1: I need to be happy with my co-workers at my good job.
Support 2: I want my family to be happy, both in life and with me.
Support 3: I want to have a fair amount of money, so we never have to worry about our basic necessities.
Thesis: My idea of a happy life involves surrounding myself with positive people and lots of money.

B. Model Essay

There are many things that go into a happy life, but I have reduced that down to three, basic things: a good job, a happy family, and a decent amount of money. I have many reasons and several examples to support my opinion.

First, a good life starts with a good job. You can do a lot of things in life: you can be a businessman, an engineer, or even a garbage collector. However, the most important thing about your job is not that you make a lot of money or become famous; rather, you just have to be content with your job. For me, I would like to have a job where I know I am making an important contribution to society. I want to be able to help people, perhaps through a non-profit organization like the Red Cross or Doctors without Borders. In addition, I would like a job knowing that I am valued; for me, that means my boss and my co-workers should be nice and pleasant to work with. It also means that they should be just as hardworking as me, so that we can help as many people as possible.

Also, I want my family to be happy. I want to be able to settle down with someone in the future and start a family with her. One of my biggest fears in life is that I will grow old with no one to talk to. If I find someone, I will want to marry her and have kids. I want to have two children, but I could also deal with having just one. Not having at least one child will make me very sad. My family should also be happy. I want to be able to provide for them, but they should want me to be around. We should be able to go to the movies together and have a good time. I don't want to argue a lot with my family at all.

Last, I want to have a fair amount of money to live off of for the rest of my life. Although I said that how much money you make from your job is not that important, it is important that you have enough money to live on. For example, I would not be happy if I couldn't pay rent on an apartment or afford to eat everyday. In that way, money does matter, but money doesn't matter so much to me once my family and I have our basic needs met. I want to be able to live fairly comfortably too; I want to be able to own a house one day and take vacations to Europe occasionally, but I don't really care if I earn a lot more other than that. I just want enough to make me and my family happy after I finish working.

To sum up, I don't want a lot out of life; I don't expect to become very rich or famous. However, I want my happy life to include a good job, a happy family, and enough money for me and my family to live off. With that, I would be content and could die happy.

C. Useful Expressions

1. There are many things that go into a happy life.

2. I have reduced that down to three basic things.

3. However, the most important thing about your job is not that you make a lot of money or become famous; rather, you just have to be content with your job.

4. However, the most important thing about your job is not that you make a lot of money or become famous; rather, you just have to be content with your job.

5. One of my biggest fears in life is that I will grow old with no one to talk to.

6. I want to have two children, but I could also deal with having just one.

7. Last, I want to have a fair amount of money to live off of for the rest of my life.

8. In that way, money does matter, but money doesn't matter so much to me once my family and I have our basic needs met.

9. To sum up, I don't want a lot out of life; I don't expect to become very rich or famous.

10. With that, I would be content and could die happy.

Q216. Which genre of books do you enjoy reading the most? Why?

A. Essay Outline

Argument: My favorite genre of books is fantasy.
Support 1: Fantasy novels always have really impressive worlds, like in Lord of the Rings.
Support 2: I really like the idea of magic.
Support 3: I really like stories about good versus evil.
Thesis: Because there are so many things I like about fantasy books, I enjoy reading them the most.

B. Model Essay

I am an avid reader; I like to read a lot of books in my free time. I read a lot of different kinds of books too, ranging from romance to science fiction to even political books. However, I enjoy reading fantasy books the most for three reasons. First, fantasy novels have really impressive worlds, like in Lord of the Rings. Second, I really like how the authors incorporate magic into their stories. Finally, I love the traditional story of good versus evil.

To start off, fantasy novels always incorporate great and diverse worlds. Take, for example, Lord of the Rings. Lord of the Rings takes place in a world called Middle Earth. There are many different kingdoms in Middle Earth, including the Elf Kingdom, where all the elves live and Mordor, where there is nothing but evil. The protagonist, Frodo, comes from the Shire, which looks like a quaint little village in the English countryside. In Lord of the Rings, there are also a big forest with tree spirits and the Misty Mountains, where there are lots of rocks and goblins. In general, the worlds in fantasy novels are so impressively described; there is just so much detail, you feel as if you are actually there. Middle Earth especially seems like a great place to have an adventure and I would love it if I had the chance to actually live in these fantasy worlds.

Next, I really like the idea of magic. It's something I always wanted to do ever since I was a little kid and something that still sticks with me today. Even though it's not real, I can do the next best thing: read fantasy novels. This is because there is always some magical element in fantasy novels. Take, for example, Harry Potter. Harry Potter was an ordinary boy who lived a miserable life in England. When he got older, he learned that he was a wizard. It is there that he starts his adventure and gets entrapped in a magical world, where he can play soccer on flying broomsticks (Quidditch) and make magic potions that can heal people or make them sick. Fantasy novels help me to escape my mundane world and let me live a fantasy, even if it's only for a couple hours.

Last, I really like fantasy novels because most of them deal with the battle between good and evil. This is a tried and true method of talking about a lot of things and it works very well; it always catches my interest. For example, in Lord of the Rings, Frodo battles many creatures who lust after his ring. The ring, made of gold, is meant to represent greed and thus, the battle for good against evil is truly a battle between greed vs. generosity. Harry Potter has the battle of Harry versus Lord Voldemort. J.K Rowling, the author of Harry Potter, has even said that Voldemort represents Adolf Hitler, and so when Harry fights Lord Voldemort, he is fighting against needless cruelty and violence. Because the triumph of good over evil is so meaningful in the fantasy genre, I love to read fantasy books.

In conclusion, the fantasy genre is my favorite among many genres. It is just one of the best because of the cool worlds created, the magic used, and the stories developed by the authors. I hope that everyone reads at least one fantasy novel before they die.

C. Useful Expressions

1. I am an avid reader; I like to read a lot of books in my free time.

2. I read a lot of different kinds of books too, ranging from romance to science fiction to even political books.

3. To start off, fantasy novels always incorporate great and diverse worlds.

4. The protagonist, Frodo, comes from the Shire, which looks like a quaint little village in the English countryside.

5. Next, I really like the idea of magic. It's something I always wanted to do ever since I was a little kid and something that still sticks with me today.

6. Even though it's not real, I can do the next best thing: read fantasy novels

7. Last, I really like fantasy novels because most of them deal with the battle between good and evil.

8. Because the triumph of good over evil is so meaningful in the fantasy genre, I love to read fantasy books.

9. In conclusion, the fantasy genre is my favorite among many genres.

10. I hope that everyone reads at least one fantasy novel before they die.

Q217. Which fruit do you like the most? Why?

A. Essay Outline

Argument: Avocados are my favorite fruit.
Support 1: Avocados are really delicious.
Support 2: Avocados come from Mexico, a country I really want to visit.
Support 3: Avocados are an unusual fruit; they're not like apples or bananas.
Thesis: Because they are unique, avocados are my favorite fruit.

B. Model Essay

Some people prefer to eat a fruit that is very sweet, like a pear, an apple, or a banana. However, I am a very different kind of person and my favorite fruit is the avocado. Not only are avocados absolutely delicious, but they come from Mexico, which is a country I really want to visit when I get older. Also, avocados are an unusual fruit, which I really like about it. Avocados are my most favorite fruit out of so many great fruits.

First of all, avocados are really delicious. They are green, but they are really creamy. They are used for a lot of different things, but my favorite thing they are used for is guacamole. Guacamole is basically a bunch of mashed up avocados with some onion, some chilies, lime juice, and cilantro. It is really delicious and it is one of the best side dishes when you go to a Mexican restaurant. Avocados are really great; because they are so creamy, some people even make ice cream out of them instead of using eggs. They make the ice cream green, but they're so good. I wish they had more avocados in Korea.

Next, avocados come from Mexico, so when I eat them, I am reminded of how much I want to go to Mexico when I am older. Even though there aren't a lot of Mexicans living in Korea right now, I have always been fascinated by Mexican culture. One of the best things that happens in Mexico is "Dia de los Muertos" or in English, "Day of the Dead." It is a time when Mexican families go to graveyards and have parties with their dead relatives. I have never been to Mexico, but this seems absolutely unique and great. Also, Dora the Explorer is from Mexico. Dora the Explorer is a very popular kid's program in the U.S. When I saw it, I was instantly hooked. Dora, the main character in Dora the Explorer, helps kids learn Spanish. Because avocados come from Mexico, one country I hope to visit when I am older, they are my favorite fruit.

Last, avocados are a very unique fruit. Unlike apples, oranges, strawberries, or bananas, avocados aren't really sweet. In fact, some people even think they are a vegetable because they are used so much in savory cuisine. Most people don't think about eating avocados after dinner. However, that is something I really like about avocados: they in some way defy traditional boundaries of what a fruit is. Even though biologically they are a fruit, it only has one massive seed that you cannot eat. They are also kind of ugly and brown on the outside, but absolutely delicious on the inside. Because the avocado is special, it is my favorite fruit.

To sum, avocados area a really great fruit that have a lot of uses. They are so different, unique, and delicious that I just love them. Plus, avocados are really great in Mexican cuisine and whenever I eat an avocado, I am reminded of Mexico. I hope to have a fiesta with my Mexican friends one day and eat a lot of avocados with them.

C. Useful Expressions

1. However, I am a very different kind of person and my favorite fruit is the avocado.

2. They are used for a lot of different things, but my favorite thing they are used for is guacamole.

3. Guacamole is basically a bunch of mashed up avocados with some onion, some chills, lime juice, and cilantro.

4. It is really delicious and it is one of the best side dishes when you go to a Mexican restaurant.

5. Next, avocados come from Mexico, so when I eat them, I am reminded of how much I want to go to Mexico when I am older.

6. Even though there aren't a lot of Mexicans living in Korea right now, I have always been fascinated by Mexican culture.

7. I have never been to Mexico, but this seems absolutely unique and great.

8. Dora the Explorer is a very popular kid's program in the U.S. When I saw it, I was instantly hooked.

9. In fact, some people even think they are a vegetable because they are used so much in savory cuisine.

10. However, that is something I really like about avocados: they in some way defy traditional boundaries of what a fruit is.

Q218. What is your favorite TV show and why?

A. Essay Outline

Argument: My favorite TV show is Downton Abbey.
Support 1: The show is about the British aristocracy in the early 1900's.
Support 2: There are many characters, and they are all very interesting.
Support 3: The costumes are very well done.
Thesis: Because Downton Abbey is a well-made TV series, it is my favorite TV show of all time.

B. Model Essay

    I don't watch a lot of television, but when I do, I try to make it count. My favorite TV show at the moment is Downton Abbey; I just started watching it and I love watching and rewatching episodes. It has quickly become my favorite show for three reasons. First, it is about the British aristocracy in the early 1900's, which to me is really fascinating. Second, there are so many three-dimensional characters, and they are all are put in very interesting circumstances. Last, the costume designers are great; their works deserve to be in a museum.

    Downton Abbey is primarily a show about aristocrats in the United Kingdom before, during, and after World War I. The series takes place in an estate called Downton Abbey and follows the lives of the rich and poor as they continue their lives in the estate. I find this time period really fascinating: it was a time of great transition in Britain, moving from an older, more hierarchical society into a more equal one. The war changed a lot of things about Britain, including the role of women in society. By watching the show, I also have gotten the chance to learn a lot more about the time period and some of the events that occurred then. I learned about the Spanish flu and British politics at the time. The series talked a lot about women's suffrage in Europe and how it affected many of the women on the show. Truly, Downton Abbey is a really interesting show and it made me very interested to learn more about British history.

    In addition, there are a lot of characters on Downton Abbey, including aristocrats and many servants and they are all very interesting. First, there is the Earl of Grantham. He is an old man, but he is very kind. He married an American woman for her money, but he still loves her. There are also their three daughters: Lady Mary, Lady Edith, and Lady Sybil. They are all very attractive, but they have very different personalities. Lady Edith, the middle child, doesn't know what to do with her life. Lady Sybil has a very strong will and Lady Mary wants to follow in her grandmother's footsteps and basically be a princess. There are a lot of servants too, like Thomas, the footman, and Mr. Bates, Lord Grantham's valet. They do not like each other at first, but they eventually learn to like each other. Mr. Bates also falls in love with Anna, one of the housemaids. They have a very beautiful, but humble, wedding. There are so many characters; it is so fascinating to see them interact with one another.

    Most importantly, though, the costumes for every episode of Downton Abbey are just fantastic. They are period pieces, true, but they look so very real and so true to what was worn back in the day. For example, Lady Mary's grandmother, the Dowager Countess of Grantham, wears a cute little tiara, while by the third season, Lady Edith starts to wear flapper dresses. My favorite, though, is the elegant black dress that Lord Grantham's wife wore. It had such a simple cut, but had lots of sparkle. It was so pretty! In truth, all the costumes are very impressive; it just looks like the costume designer had a lot of fun designing, sewing, and making all of the costumes.

Because of the wonderful characters, costumes and story material, Downton Abbey is simply a marvelous show and absolutely my favorite show on television currently. Everything about this TV show is just done perfectly. I hope everyone gets the chance to watch this great show.

C. Useful Expressions

1. I don't watch a lot of television, but when I do, I try to make it count.

2. Second, there are so many three-dimensional characters, and they are all are put in very interesting circumstances.

3. The series takes place in an estate called Downton Abbey and follows the lives of the rich and poor as they continue their lives in the estate.

4. The series talked a lot about women's suffrage in Europe and how it affected many of the women on the show.

5. I find this time period really fascinating: it was a time of great transition in Britain, moving from an older, more hierarchical society into a more equal one.

6. By watching the show, I also have gotten the chance to learn a lot more about the time period and some of the events that occurred then.

7. Most importantly, though, the costumes for every episode of Downton Abbey are just fantastic.

8. They are period pieces, true, but they look so very real and so true to what was worn back in the day.

9. In truth, all the costumes are very impressive; it just looks like the costume designer had a lot of fun designing, sewing, and making all of the costumes.

10. Everything about this TV show is just done perfectly.

> **Q219. What is your favorite movie and why?**

A. Essay Outline

Argument: Spirited Away is my favorite movie.
Support 1: It was directed by Hayao Miyazaki, who is a great animator and director.
Support 2: It is beautifully animated; I love all of the colors in the film.
Support 3: The story is great, interesting, and thought-provoking.
Thesis: Because Spirited Away is such a great movie, it is my favorite movie.

B. Model Essay

Spirited Away is one of the best movies made in the 21st century. Directed by Hayao Miyazaki, it tells the story of a little girl named Chihiro who gets lost in an alternate universe where spirits run and inhabit a magical bathhouse. The film, made in 2001, won many awards; it even won Best Animated Feature at the 75th Annual Academy Awards. Because it is beautifully animated, tells a great story, and was directed by the great Hayao Miyazaki, Spirited Away is my favorite film ever made.

One of the greatest animators ever, Hayao Miyazaki, wrote and directed this masterpiece of cinema. Miyazaki was known before Spirited Away for some great works like Laputa: Castle in the Sky, Princess Mononoke, My Neighbor Totoro, and Kiki's Delivery Service. Miyazaki always makes animated films featuring children, but adults can definitely enjoy the films as well. His films always have some sort of magical element, either ghosts or spirits or magical, talking animals. They take place in magical worlds where curiosity and idealism are rewarded. At the same time, many of the children have to face difficult challenges like saving an entire forest or people. Because Miyazaki is such a brilliant director, his touch transforms Spirited Away from a good film to one of my favorites.

Another reason I love Spirited Away is the fact that it is animated with such craft. Unlike Miyazaki's earlier films, which were limited by technology, Spirited Away is really the first film by Miyazaki where the colors shine and the figures float so easily. There is so much detail paid to everything from hair to simple objects. Even compared to Miyazaki's earlier films, the faces have so much more emotion and depth. Even the images seem to move with such grace; to a certain extent, it doesn't even feel like we're watching a series of images, but an authentic, real video. Because Spirited Away is so well-made and every character and image is so great, it is my absolute favorite film.

All of this pales in comparison to the basic story of Spirited Away. Spirited Away revolves around a girl named Chihiro. She and her parents are moving to a new place and Chihiro is not excited to go. They end up at an abandoned amusement park; Chihiro's parents eat at a restaurant stand and are instantly turned into pigs. It then becomes Chihiro's task to try and save them from forever being pigs in the spirit world. Without revealing too much more of the story, Chihiro metaphorically has to learn to become an adult. She has to face many more difficult tasks along with way, including cleaning up a very smelly, polluted river spirit. Spirited Away is a highly fascinating coming-of-age tale that makes you think about what it means to become an adult and the future of the world.

In conclusion, Spirited Away is a fantastic movie that makes you think about a lot of things. It was directed by the great Hayao Miyazaki, known for many different great films. It is a very beautiful film too, with so many lush colors and seamless transitions, but these only help the fact that the story is so magnificently written and wonderfully understated. It is for these reasons that Spirited Away is my most cherished movie. I hope that everyone can see this movie one day.

C. Useful Expressions

1. One of the greatest animators ever, Hayao Miyazaki, wrote and directed this masterpiece of cinema.

2. His films always have some sort of magical element, either ghosts or spirits or magical, talking animals.

3. They take place in magical worlds where curiosity and idealism are rewarded.

4. Because Miyazaki is such a brilliant director, his touch transforms Spirited Away from a good film to one of my favorites.

5. Another reason I love Spirited Away is the fact that it is animated with such craft.

6. There is so much detail paid to everything from hair to simple objects.

7. Even the images seem to move with such grace; to a certain extent, it doesn't even feel like we're watching a series of images, but an authentic, real video.

8. They end up at an abandoned amusement park; Chihiro's parents eat at a restaurant stand and are instantly turned into pigs.

9. Without revealing too much more of the story, Chihiro metaphorically has to learn to become an adult.

10. Spirited Away is a highly fascinating coming-of-age tale that makes you think about what it means to become an adult and the future of the world.

> **Q220. Compare the advantages and the disadvantages of Smart Phones.**

A. Essay Outline

Argument: Smart Phones have changed the world we know in some positive ways, but they have also affected the world in some negative ways.
Support 1: Let me begin with the positives aspects of the Smart Phone: convenience, emergency use, and information tool.
Support 2: Now, I will discuss the negatives that come from the Smart Phone usage: distractions while operating machinery, addiction, and health risks.
Support 3: In my opinion, Smart Phones are a vital tool in this technologically advanced world.
Thesis: To summarize, Smart Phones have both detrimental factors and advantageous factors.

B. Model Essay

Nowadays, almost everyone in the USA has some sort of mobile phone. However, a large percentage of people use what is now known as a Smart Phone. Smart Phones have changed the world we know in some positive ways, but they have also affected the world in some negative ways. These intelligent phones provide us not only with a source of calling people, but also a way to browse the Internet, to take photos, and to save important information all at our fingertips.

Let me begin with the positives aspects of the Smart Phone. The most obvious plus to this tool is that it is more convenient to get a hold of somebody. In the past, we had to call somebody's home and leave a message for them. However, nowadays, we are able to call their cell phone and reach them immediately. Also, in an emergency situation, Smart Phones are a vital tool for fast response. The biggest factor that sets the Smart Phone apart from regular mobile phones is the fact that we can stay in the know about many things. All Smart Phones have the ability to access the Internet, and as you know, the Internet has a plethora of information.

Now, I will discuss the negatives that come from the Smart Phone usage. The biggest and most troublesome downside of the Smart Phone is that it is distracting. While people are driving, they will talk on their phone, text their friends, or post a recent update on their Facebook account. These distractions often times lead to vehicular accidents or people walking into a hazard. Another adverse effect is that they become highly addictive. As students, we want to text our friends or play a game during class, instead of focusing on our teacher's instructions. Furthermore, it distracts us from doing our necessary tasks in life, because we want to beat a game, or to always update our friends through our desired social media network. Probably the most unknown negative is the medical hazards it can pose to us. Research has been conducted on the increased use of technology, specifically Smart Phones, and it has shown that they cause bad posture, poor eyesight, and they even can impair younger children's thinking skills.

In my opinion, Smart Phones are a vital tool in this technologically advanced world. However, I do think that the Smart Phone is taking over too much. Recently I bought my first Smart Phone, and I have now become one of those addicted people, too. I always feel I have to have my cellphone next to me, just in case something important happens. On the other hand though, I love the fact that my Smart Phone is my camera, phone, calendar, and my clock all in one. So despite the negatives, I would never give up my Smart

Phone. I can recall a time when I had to carry around multiple devices or tools to accomplish all those tasks. So, I am not completely opposed to the intelligent phone's usage. I just feel that our brains should be the ones doing the thinking, not the phone.

To summarize, Smart Phones have both detrimental factors and advantageous factors. The negatives range from being a distraction to being harmful to our health. The positives range from giving us a multiple-device-tool-in-one to having a first responder at our fingertips in an emergency situation. Over the next decade, I am sure that the Smart Phone will continue to change. I just hope that we can maintain our own intelligence and not allow the phone to do all the work for us.

C. Useful Expressions

1. Nowadays, almost everyone in the USA has some sort of mobile phone.

2. However, a large percentage of people use what is now known as a Smart Phone.

3. The most obvious plus to this tool is that it is more convenient to get a hold of somebody.

4. The biggest factor that sets the Smart Phone apart from regular mobile phones is the fact that we can stay in the know about many things.

5. The biggest and most troublesome downside of the Smart Phone is that it is distracting.

6. Another adverse effect is that they become highly addictive.

7. However, I do think that the Smart Phone is taking over too much.

8. So despite the negatives, I would never give up my Smart Phone.

9. So, I am not completely opposed to the intelligent phone's usage.

10. The negatives range from being a distraction to being harmful to our health.

Q221. Which option is healthier, eating three large meals a day or eating four to five small meals a day?

A. Essay Outline

Argument: Eating many smaller meals throughout the day is better than eating a few larger meals.
Support 1: Eating smaller meals is healthier, if and only if they are properly balanced meals
Support 2: By eating a small meal every four hours during the day time, our bodies can be supplied with a constant flow of energy.
Support 3: Eating four to five well-balanced meals throughout the day can curb your hunger and lead to maintaining a healthy weight.
Thesis: Eating smaller meals more often throughout the day has been proven to make us feel less sleepy, maintain a balanced weight, and it curbs our desire to eat more.

B. Model Essay

In life, we have many decisions to make that affect our health. One of the decisions is about what we eat, how much we eat, and how often we eat. According to a study conducted in 1989, by David Jenkins, M.D., Ph.D., and Tom Wolever, M.D., Ph.D., of the University of Toronto, it is better for our health to eat five or six meals a day, rather than to eat three meals a day. So, I must agree with the doctors that eating many smaller meals throughout the day is better than eating a few larger meals for various reasons: it reduces our calorie intake, keeps our level of insulin up, and controls our hunger.

First, let me explain what the smaller meals should consist of, in order to make it clear why eating these types of meals is healthier for us. Eating smaller meals is healthier, if and only if they are properly balanced meals, such as apples and peanut butter, versus a candy bar and milkshake. To achieve this proper balance, each smaller meal should include a low-fat or lean protein, a fiber, and at least one fruit or vegetable. An unusual thing that should be implemented into this type of meal is a healthy fat. This may sound quiet odd, but some examples of healthy fats are avocados, nuts, and fatty fish. Eating a balanced meal is the key to why the smaller meal diet works as a healthier option.

Secondly, I will explain what eating four to five smaller meals can do to our chemical make-up inside of our bodies. To begin with, many people often get sleepy around three to four in the afternoon. Why is this? It's because our glucose levels have dropped, which lowers our insulin level. Most people go for six hours without eating, so it's no wonder we feel lethargic by the time the afternoon reaches us. By eating a small meal every four hours during the day time, our bodies can be supplied with a constant flow of energy. Also, multiple meals have been proven to lower our cholesterol, which is why many doctors suggest a diet, such as this, to reduce our cholesterol levels.

Finally, I will discuss how eating four to five well-balanced meals throughout the day can curb your hunger and lead to maintaining a healthy weight. It is mostly due to the fact that eating more often makes us feel less hungry. This is because we have a constant flow of food in our bodies. This then in return helps to increase our metabolism, which is one of the factors to maintaining a healthy weight. The smaller meal more frequently regime also helps reduce our calorie intake, because if we feel full for a longer period of time, then we are less likely to snack on the 'unhealthy' foods in-between our regular more frequent meals.

Despite the fact that eating more frequently could actually mean less nutrition and more calories if you don't carefully plan out your snacks and meals, it still provides our bodies with the needed energy and numerous benefits. Eating smaller meals more often throughout the day has been proven to make us feel less sleepy, maintain a balanced weight, and it curbs our desire to eat more. My suggestion to everyone is to follow this method if they want to live a long and happy life. Also, who doesn't want to eat more delicious food more often!

C. Useful Expressions

1. According to a study conducted in 1989 by David Jenkins, M.D., Ph.D., and Tom Wolever, M.D., Ph.D., of the University of Toronto, they have proven that it is better for our health to eat five or six meals a day, rather than to eat three meals a day.

2. So, I must agree with the doctor that eating many smaller meals throughout the day is better than eating a few larger meals for various reasons; it reduces our calorie intake, keeps our level of insulin up, and controls our hunger.

3. First, let me explain what the smaller meals should consist of, in order to make it clear why eating these types of meals is healthier for us.

4. Eating smaller meals is healthier, if and only if they are properly balanced meals, such as apples and peanut butter, versus a candy bar and milkshake.

5. Most people go for six hours without eating, so it's no wonder we feel lethargic by the time the afternoon reaches us.

6. Also, multiple meals have been proven to lower our cholesterol, which is why many doctors suggest a diet, such as this, to reduce our cholesterol levels.

7. Finally, I will discuss how eating four to five well-balanced meals throughout the day can curb your hunger and lead to maintaining a healthy weight.

Q222. If you could win a lot of money, how much would you want to win and why?

A. Essay Outline

Argument: If I were given a lot of money, I would want to win 200 million dollars.
Support 1: The first reason I would want 200 million dollars is because I would want to use half of my winnings by donating it to a local charity or orphanage.
Support 2: Second, I would use a large portion of the remaining 100 million dollars to travel around the world for an entire year.
Support 3: Finally, I would want just a small chunk of money for my own personal gain, maybe 50,000 dollars.
Thesis: Having too much money would be overwhelming, and having too little money would be a disappointment; therefore by receiving 200 million dollars, I could do great things for others, while also getting a little benefit for myself.

B. Model Essay

If I were given the chance to win a lot of money, I would want to win 200 million dollars. I would want this much money because I could donate my money to a local charity. Then, I could travel around the world while volunteering at needy schools and hospitals. Finally, I would want to do something for myself, such as buying a new computer.

The first reason I would want 200 million dollars is because I would want to use half of my winnings by donating it to a local charity or orphanage. I know that there are many places that could use more resources to do good things for others. So why do I need to be having excess amounts of money when there are needy people out there? There are many orphanages and soup kitchens here in Daegu, and I know that their visitors and residents will benefit greatly from the donation. If I received only a small amount of money, I couldn't do as much good for this specific community.

Second, I would use a large portion of the remaining 100 million dollars to travel around the world for an entire year. I want to go to Australia, Asia, and Europe the most. While in these new countries, I would do volunteer work and donate my time and money to help them build more schools or hospitals. I have done volunteer work already at local schools in America that needed a lot of help. It was very tough work, but it was also very rewarding to see those students' faces light up when they saw how their run down school was completely changed. So, by winning a large sum of money, I could do more beneficial work around the world.

Finally, I would want just a small chunk of money for my own personal gain, maybe 50,000 dollars. My computer is very old and it does not have enough memory for all of the photos I take. By buying a new computer, I would be able to take more pictures and organize them better. I love taking photos, so it would brighten my life greatly. I could also update my wardrobe, buy some new books, and fly my family to Korea to see me.

Having too much money would be overwhelming, and having too little money would be a disappointment. So by doing by receiving 200 million dollars, I could do great things for others, while also getting a little benefit for myself. We are all entitled to a little splurge once and a while, so why not dream big, and do random acts of kindness for others at the same time?

C. Useful Expressions

1. The first reason I would want 200 million dollars is because I would want to use half of my winnings by donating it to a local charity or orphanage.

2. There are many orphanages and soup kitchens here in Daegu, and I know that their visitors and residents will benefit greatly from the donation.

3. Second, I would use a large portion of the remaining 100 million dollars to travel around the world for an entire year.

4. It was very tough work, but it was also very rewarding to see those students' faces light up when they saw how their run down school was completely changed.

5. Finally, I would want just a small chunk of money for my own personal gain, maybe 50,000 dollars.

6. I love taking photos, so it would brighten my life greatly.

7. Having too much money would be overwhelming, and having too little money would be a disappointment.

8. We are all entitled to a little splurge once and a while, so why not dream big, and do random acts of kindness for others at the same time.

Q223. We are continuously learning and doing new things in life and often times we fail at our first attempt. Describe your first attempt to gain something new.

A. Essay Outline

Argument: A very funny experience happened to me during my first attempt to gain knowledge about cooking potatoes by myself.
Support 1: My mother entrusted each of her young children to cook dinner for the rest of the family.
Support 2: Something went very wrong though in the process of trying to cook potatoes.
Support 3: I learned a few great lessons from this.
Thesis: So my first attempt to learn how to cook something as simple as potatoes, also taught me other important life lessons.

B. Model Essay

A very funny experience happened to me during my first attempt to gain knowledge about cooking potatoes for myself. Usually, scary cooking experiences don't happen until around the high school ages, but mine happened when I was much younger, in elementary school. I definitely gained something from this experience that I will never forget.

To start with, I was eight years old and at home with my two sisters, who were six and ten. My mom always trusted us to cook dinner and to have it ready for her when she came home. She felt that it was a very good trait for children to have for us to be independent. Plus, my mom was very busy working in order to afford raising her three children on her own. So, it was my turn to cook the potatoes for the first time. I turned on the oven and put the potatoes in, just like my mom had shown me many times.

However, something went horribly wrong. The potatoes suddenly burst into flames. I was very nervous at first. However, I calmly and quickly called my mom hoping she wasn't going to be angry. She told me in her soothing, motherly voice, to carefully pour baking powder onto the flames. The flames immediately went out and I cleaned up the mess before my mom came home.

Even though this was a frightening experience, I learned some very important lessons. I learned how to remain calm, and to think clearly in a time of panic. It has helped through many of my life's challenges. I am very thankful for my mother's encouragement of independence. I have used many of the skills as an adult that I had learned as a child.

So my first attempt to learn how to cook something as simple as potatoes also taught me other important life lessons. I still don't know why the potatoes burst into flames. It will forever be a mystery to us all. The most valuable lesson to take away from this experience was to remain calm, call for help, and to not make the same mistake again.

C. Useful Expressions

1. A very funny experience happened to me during my first attempt to gain knowledge about cooking potatoes for myself.

2. Usually, scary cooking experiences don't happen until around the high school ages, but mine happened when I was much younger, in elementary school.

3. I definitely gained something from this experience that I will never forget.

4. She felt that it was a very good trait for children to have for us to be independent.

5. I turned on the oven, and put the potatoes in, just like my mom had shown me many times.

6. However, something went horribly wrong.

7. I was very nervous at first.

8. Even though this was a frightening experience, I learned some very important lessons.

9. I learned how to remain calm, and to think clearly in a time of panic.

10. It will forever be a mystery to us all.

Q224. Describe your ideal holiday resort.

A. Essay Outline

Argument: My ideal holiday resort would have to be in a place that is hot and tropical, such as the Grand Cayman Islands.
Support 1: It is located in the Caribbean Sea near Jamaica, so the weather is perfect.
Support 2: Besides the weather, the scenery is beautiful.
Support 3: There are many interesting places to visit.
Thesis: The warm waters and the perfect weather make the Grand Cayman Islands my ideal holiday resort.

B. Model Essay

There are many locations to construct a holiday resort at, such as Japan, China, South Korea, and the USA. However, my ideal holiday resort would have to be in a place that is hot, tropical, and not somewhere I've lived for a long time already at. Therefore, the best place for me to stay at a holiday resort would be the Grand Cayman Islands.

To start with, the Grand Cayman Island is a fairly small island located in the Caribbean Sea, near Jamaica. Therefore, the weather there is perfect. When I visited these islands last December to help babysit my cousin's three children, I found this fact out for myself. The temperature only differs by no more than 10 degrees from the day time to the night time. Plus, there is always a cool breeze blowing that acts as an air-conditioner to warm sun heated air.

Besides the weather, the scenery is also beautiful! The crystal clear blue water meets a clean white sand beach. Usually, I don't like going into the ocean or sea because it is so cold. However, the water surrounding the Grand Cayman Islands is like bath water! The main attraction is the seven mile beach, where most of the hotels are built. It gives almost every visitor a great view of the tropical serenity. I like to enjoy my holiday by sitting on the beach, with a nice cool drink, and watching the scenery change throughout the day.

On top of the great weather and beautiful scenery, there are interesting places to visit. Since it is a British colonized tropical island, there is a lot of history to learn and to see around the island. Plus, it is the perfect place to go scuba diving, where you can swim with the stingrays and tour the underwater ship wrecks. Also, you can go on a pirate ship and be treated like one of the crew, having to clean the deck with a toothbrush. The Grand Cayman Island is not a big island, but it offers so many great things to do.

The warm waters and the perfect weather make the Grand Cayman Islands my ideal holiday resort. The island has a great many of places to see, and also many exciting things to do. I know that if I had the chance to go again, I would leave immediately with no hesitations!

C. Useful Expressions

1. When I visited these islands last December to help babysit my cousin's three children, I found this fact out for myself.

2. The temperature only differs by no more than 10 degrees from the day time to the night time.

3. Plus, there is always a cool breeze blowing that acts as an air-conditioner to warm sun heated air.

4. Besides the weather, the scenery is also beautiful! The crystal clear blue water meets a clean white sand beach.

5. The main attraction is the seven mile beach, where most of the hotels are built.

6. On top of the great weather and beautiful scenery, there are the interesting places to visit.

7. Since it is a British colonized tropical island, there is a lot of history to learn and to see around the island.

8. The Grand Cayman Island is not a big island, but it offers so many great things to do.

9. The island has a great many of places to see, and also many exciting things to do.

10. I know that if I had the chance to go again, I would leave immediately with no hesitations!

Q225. What is your biggest ambition in life?

A. Essay Outline

Argument: My biggest ambition in life is to open my own early childhood education center.
Support 1: I love being around children and I have had a lot of experience with early childhood.
Support 2: I hope to nurture the children at their most formidable ages.
Support 3: It will take a lot of work to make this dream come true.
Thesis: Because it will be so rewarding, I want to open my own early childhood education center.

B. Model Essay

I have many ambitions in life to do many great things, such as get married and have a family, win the lottery, travel the world, and eat live octopus. However, my biggest ambition in life is to open my own early childhood education center. This will be a big feat to me because it will take a lot of time, preparation, finances, and other resources to make it run successfully. However, it is something I am willing to put a lot of hard work into because teaching children is my passion.

First, I have this ambition because I love to be around children. Also, my educational specialty is in dealing with early childhood aged children. Ever since I was young, I have always babysat or taught children in some manner. I started to teach at my church when I was 13 years old and immediately fell in love with it. So by doing this, I will be continuing on with my life's passion.

Next, by opening this education center, I hope to nurture the children at their most formidable ages. In this type of environment, the children will learn to have manners and to respect others. They will also learn the basic life skills needed in life, such as brushing their teeth, cleaning the dishes, and sharing with others. These vital skills of how to treat others will guide my future students a long way in their lives. Just imagine what properly raised and educated children could do to change our world, versus the children who are raised without ever hearing the word 'no'.

However, in order to achieve this great ambition of mine, I will have to save a lot of money, and also start to network with people. These people will be able to help support me financially and in many other ways. I'm already starting to save money, and I hope that by the time I am in my 40s or 50s, I will have enough money to make my dream come true.

Hard work is usually involved when you have great ambitions to do something. So it is no surprise to me that opening my own education center will take a lot of work on my part. In the long run, I know that it will be a great experience for the children who will attend my education center. I hope that with the right support and through the right people, I can accomplish this grand goal.

C. Useful Expressions

1. This will be a big feat to me because it will take a lot of time, preparation, finances, and other resources to make it run successfully.

2. However, it is something I am willing to put a lot of hard work into because teaching children is my passion.

3. Ever since I was young, I have always babysat or taught children in some manner.

4. Next, by opening this education center, I hope to nurture the children at their most formidable ages.

5. These vital skills of how to treat others will guide my future students a long way in their lives.

6. Just imagine what properly raised and educated children could do to change our world, versus the children who are raised without ever hearing the word 'no'.

7. However, in order to achieve this great ambition of mine, I will have to save a lot of money, and also start to network with people.

8. Hard work is usually involved when you have great ambitions to do something.

9. So it is no surprise to me that opening my own education center will take a lot of work on my part.

Q226. Which family member has influenced you the most? Why is this person a positive or negative role model in your life?

A. Essay Outline

Argument: The person who has influenced me the most is my older sister for many reasons.
Support 1: She is the person I have been around the most since the day I was born.
Support 2: She was not necessarily a good influence on my life though.
Support 3: I learned from those mistakes that she made and decided to never do them myself,
Thesis: My older sister taught me what not to do and I will forever be grateful for her guidance to stay out of trouble.

B. Model Essay

Many superior people have influenced me positively and negatively throughout my life. However, the family member who has influenced me the most is my older sister. She influenced me in an unusual way though.

Firstly, my older sister is the person I have been around since the day I was born. Therefore, she is naturally the person who would have the most power and influence over my life. For the first 15 years of my life, we lived in the same room, went to the same school, and went everywhere else together. I was called her 'mini-me' because we never left each other's side. Sometimes, I didn't like this type of attention because I never felt like my own person next to her.

Normally, this closeness would bring about a positive influence, but she had quite the opposite effect on me. Actually, she taught me all the bad things not to do because I saw her make many mistakes. She would stay out late, talk back to our parents, and just push every limit that was set by any authority. Most children would follow in their big sisters footsteps and do the same things that their 'role-model' does. For me, if I followed in her footsteps, I would have been in an enormous amount of trouble too.

However, I learned from those mistakes that she made and decided that I should never do them too. This is because I did not like the punishments and treatment she had received from our parents. I had seen how severely she was punished for doing all those bad things, and it made me do the opposite of everything she did. One example was when she came home late, which happened often. This time, our mother caught her and she was grounded for 2 months. I loved hanging out with my friends, so I never came home late because my older sister set the example of what not to do.

It is unusual to think that the person who has influenced me the most is not a positive influence. Sometimes, negative things in our lives teach us more than the positive things in our lives. My older sister taught me what not to do and I will forever be grateful for her guidance to stay out of trouble.

C. Useful Expressions

1. Many superior people have influenced me positively and negatively throughout my life.

2. Therefore, she is naturally the person who would have the most power and influence over my life.

3. Sometimes, I didn't like this type of attention because I never felt like my own person next to her.

4. Normally, this closeness would bring about a positive influence, but she had quite the opposite effect on me.

5. She would stay out late, talk back to our parents, and just push every limit that was set by any authority.

6. For me, if I followed in her footsteps, I would have been in an enormous amount of trouble too.

7. I had seen how severely she was punished for doing all those bad things, and it made me do the opposite of everything she did.

8. I loved hanging out with my friends, so I never came home late, because my older sister set the example of what not to do.

9. Sometimes, negative things in our lives teach us more than the positive things in our lives.

10. My older sister taught me what not to do and I will forever be grateful for her guidance to stay out of trouble.

> **Q227. Where do you see yourself in twenty years?**

A. Essay Outline

Argument: In twenty years, I hope to see myself with a family, settled down in a home somewhere, and teaching.
Support 1: To me, having a family is the most important thing that I want in my future.
Support 2: Having my own place will increase my level of happiness.
Support 3: Having a stable teaching job is something that I long for.
Thesis: In twenty years, I hope to see myself with a family, settled down in a home somewhere, and teaching, because by having all of these things, I will have achieved my perfect life and level of happiness.

B. Model Essay

I don't know what my future really holds for me but I hope that it will be just as good as or even better than the life I have now. In twenty years, I hope to see myself with a family, settled down in a home somewhere, and teaching. By having all of these things, I will have achieved my perfect life and level of happiness.

To begin with, having my own family is the most important thing that I want in my future. Currently, I am not dating anybody, but I hope that one day that will change for me. Having a family of my own is something that I have desired to have for a long time and I know it will eventually come with patience. I want a family that is close and supportive of each other. Also I want a family who shows unconditional love but also shows tough love. A family is the group of people who will guide you in the right direction, but will always take you back if you stray from the path.

Next, having my own place will increase my level of happiness. This is because I won't have to share my living space with other people who don't respect shared living spaces. Also, I won't feel like I always have to clean up after people who are not my own family. When I have my own family, I will have no issues cleaning up after them. However, I will teach them to clean the dishes after using them, to wipe off the counter if they spill, and to take out the trash on a regular basis. These basic skills are very useful when we become adults who are living on their own or in a shared living experience at college.

Lastly, I hope to be teaching in twenty years. I love teaching and it is something I know I am good at. When you are good at something, why not continue doing it? Therefore, I will continue to work hard at my special skill and improve upon my techniques through various classes and courses that will be offered to me. I hope to be in a university professor position by then or running my educational business. It is an achievable goal, but it will take time to make it happen.

We don't know exactly what the future really holds for us, but I hope that mine will be just as good as or even better than the life I have now. In twenty years, I hope to see myself with a family, settled down in a home somewhere, and teaching. By having all of these things, I will have achieved my perfect life and level of happiness.

C. Useful Expressions

1. I don't know what my future really holds for me but I hope that it will be just as good as or even better than the life I have now.

2. In twenty years, I hope to see myself with a family, settled down in a home somewhere, and teaching.

3. Currently, I am not dating anybody, but I hope that one day that will change for me.

4. Also I want a family who shows unconditional love but also shows tough love.

5. A family is the group of people who will guide you in the right direction, but will always take you back if you stray from the path.

6. Also I won't feel like I always have to clean up after people who are not my own family.

7. When you are good at something, why not continue doing it?

8. Therefore, I will continue to work hard at my special skill and improve upon my techniques through various classes and courses that will be offered to me.

9. It is an achievable goal, but it will take time to make it happen.

Q228. What quality or qualities do you look for in a best friend?

A. Essay Outline

Argument: A best friend should have some specific qualities; honest and trustworthy, understanding, and supportive.
Support 1: Without having an honest friend, there can be no trust.
Support 2: The next, understanding, is also a very important quality to have in a best friend.
Support 3: The last quality I want in a best friend is support.
Thesis: Since honesty and trust, understanding, and support are all essential aspects of a long lasting and strong friendship, I want a best friend that possesses all of the aforementioned characteristics.

B. Model Essay

Throughout our lives, we meet many people who come and go. Some of them become friends, some become mistakes, and some become best friends. No matter what happens between these relationships, they all teach us lessons. However, a best friend should have some specific qualities; she should be honest and trustworthy, understanding, and supportive. Without these qualities, there isn't much of a friendship, let alone a relationship that is one of the closest we have in our lives.

First and foremost, honesty and trust go hand in hand. Without having an honest friend, there can be no trust. For example, if Sue knows something that could prevent John from being hurt, she should tell John immediately, no matter how hurtful it could be. If Sue doesn't say something and he finds out that his friend knew about it, it will be detrimental to their friendship's trust. How can you trust somebody who isn't fully honest with you? Often times, so-called-friends withhold information in fear of it hurting you, but it hurts more when it was something trivial that should have been told in the first place.

The next, understanding, is also a very important quality to have in a best friend. A best friend is supposed to be the person that knows you the most and is by your side at all times. So, they should be able to understand that you are going through a difficult time and give you the space and understanding that you need. Sometimes, something negative happens between friends, and all they need is just a little bit of distance. But, when a friend continues to leave notes and pester the person, it leads to even more resentment towards the person who did wrong in the first place. Best friends understand this balance, and they don't continue to pressure you into talking, until you are ready to do so.

The last quality I want in a best friend is support. When we are being faced with challenging decisions in life, we need a rock to lean on. Your best friend is supposed to be that rock. They are somebody who can talk to, cry to, and laugh with about all the pros and cons of that decision. For example, when deciding to move to a foreign country, the best friend might want to be selfish to keep their friend in the same country as them. However, they will be supportive and give them an open ear to bounce off their ideas and thoughts to.

I have many friends, but only two of them I consider to be a best friend. They all possess these basic qualities; honesty and trust, understanding, and support. I couldn't imagine a life without my best friends or a life with friends who didn't stand by my side, even while I'm thousands of miles away in a foreign country for an extended period of time.

C. Useful Expressions

1. Some of them become friends, some become mistakes, and some become best friends.

2. No matter what happens between these relationships, they all teach us lessons.

3. Without these qualities, there isn't much of a friendship, let alone a relationship that is one of the closest we have in our lives.

4. First and foremost, honesty and trust go hand in hand.

5. If Sue doesn't say something and he finds out that his friend knew about it, it will be detrimental to their friendship's trust.

6. Often times, so-called-friends withhold information in fear of it hurting you, but it hurts more when it was something trivial that should have been told in the first place.

7. But, when a friend continues to leave notes and pester the person, it leads to even more resentment towards the person who did wrong in the first place.

8. When we are being faced with challenging decisions in life, we need a rock to lean on.

9. They are somebody who can talk to, cry to, and laugh with about all the pros and cons of that decision.

10. However, they will be supportive and give them an open ear to bounce off their ideas and thoughts to.

Q229. Parents should be required to pay for their children's university education. Do you agree or disagree with this statement?

A. Essay Outline

Argument: Parents should not pay for their children's university education.
Support 1: Paying for one's higher education teaches students who have entered adulthood to be financially responsible.
Support 2: A university student can be more academically responsible.
Support 3: Parents can still choose to support their child financially later.
Thesis: Despite the negatives of being overwhelmed by the financial burden of loans, paying for one's own university education has many positives.

B. Model Essay

    In many countries, parents pay for their children's higher education in its entirety. In other countries, the university student must take out numerous loans. Which of this is the correct point of view? It's a rather difficult question to answer because I feel it should be a balance between the two. However, if I had to choose to agree or disagree with the statement, 'parents should pay for their children's university education', I would choose the latter.

    In the first place, paying for ones higher education teaches students who have entered adulthood to be financially responsible. While students are in universities, they are still able to reach out to their parents for assistance, as well as after their graduation. However, here they are eligible for low-interest loans, scholarships, and other sources of income. So, by having a university student pay for education, they can build their credit score, as well as their confidence to survive in a financial environment.

    Second, a university student can be more academically responsible. I paid for my own degree, and I worked very hard to get all A's in my classes. So I know from first-hand experience that it teaches academic responsibility to people. When somebody pays for something on their own, they are more apt to treat it well. The same goes for paying for one's university degree. Many times, university students view college as a party place, and not much of an academic environment. However, having responsibility for the bill ensures that they take their classes seriously, attend them all, and complete all of the requirements for their courses.

    Third, parents can still choose to support their child financially later. After a student graduates with a university degree, the parents can give their child a check for a graduation gift to help with the overwhelming loans that built up over the last four years. I know people who have over 100,000 dollars in college loans, and this can be very stressful to them when they are required to start paying it back. I fortunately worked hard and paid off all of my college loans because I had a few jobs while I attended my university.

    In summary, despite the negatives of being overwhelmed by the financial burden of loans, paying for one's own university education has many positives. It teaches financial responsibility, as well as academic responsibility. The financial responsibility learned in the college years will last long into the adult years. Also, just because the parents don't pay for the university education for their children while they attend college, it doesn't mean that they can't help out after they have graduated and after their child has learned the vital lessons that come from these formidable years.

C. Useful Expressions

1. In many countries, parents pay for their children's higher education in its entirety.

2. However, if I had to choose to agree or disagree with the statement, 'parents should pay for their children's university education', I would choose the latter.

3. While students are in universities, they are still able to reach out to their parents for assistance, as well as after their graduation.

4. So, by having a university student pay for their education, they can build their credit score, as well as their confidence to survive in a financial environment.

5. So I know from first-hand experience that it teaches academic responsibility to people.

6. When somebody pays for something on their own, they are more apt to treat it well.

7. The same goes for paying for one's university degree.

8. Many times, university students view college as a party place, and not much of an academic environment.

9. The financial responsibility learned in the college years will last long into the adult years.

10. Also, just because the parents don't pay for the university education for their children while they attend college, it doesn't mean that they can't help out after they have graduated, and after their child has learned the vital lessons that come from these formidable years.

Q230. Describe the qualities of a good citizen.

A. Essay Outline

Argument: There are three very important qualities that I deem to be required in a good citizen; they should be a faithful voter, they should never break the law, and they should always pay their expected taxes.

Support 1: First off, they should be a faithful voter.

Support 2: Second, a good citizen is someone who never breaks the law.

Support 3: The third quality to be considered as a good citizen is that a person should pay their taxes and pay them on time.

Thesis: Since the above mentioned qualities are all supportive of making a better community, I feel that voting, being a law abiding citizen, and paying our required taxes show that we are good citizens.

B. Model Essay

We are all citizens in a country somewhere, but what makes us good citizens? There are three very important qualities that I deem to be required in a good citizen. They are that they should be a faithful voter, they should never break the law, and they should always pay their expected taxes.

First off, they should be a faithful voter. What does being a faithful voter mean? It means that they should vote in every election. This ensures that their voice is heard and the right officials are being elected into office. If they do not vote in an election, then I feel that they don't have the right to speak their mind about the elected officials because they didn't vote for anybody. It frustrates me when somebody who didn't vote complains about their government. I always say to them, "Vote and do something about it. It's our right as citizens!"

Second, a good citizen is someone who never breaks the law. What I mean by this is that they should never cheat, steal, kill, or damage anybody else's property. Good citizens should be moral role models for the youth in the community. If they break the laws, then they are setting an immoral example for future generations. The future generations will think it is ok to behave badly, and then the community will turn into a dangerous place to live. If we are good role models for future generations, then we can build a great country to live in.

The third quality to be considered a good citizen is that a person should pay their taxes and pay them on time. By paying taxes on time, we are giving money back to the community. This tax money, in theory, goes to the schools, the police force, parks, etc. If we don't pay them or don't pay them on time, then our communities will not have ample resources to provide the best possible place to live. I know it seems like paying taxes is a burden and unfair sometimes, but they do truly help our communities become a better place.

Since the above mentioned qualities are all supportive of making a better community, I feel that voting, being a law-abiding citizen, and paying our required taxes show that we are good citizens. We should all strive to be good citizens, and these three aspects are just simple ways we can be exactly that. If we do not follow these simple guidelines, then we are doing the opposite and should be punished appropriately by the law.

C. Useful Expressions

1. There are three very important qualities that I deem to be required in a good citizen.

2. This ensures that their voice is heard and the right officials are being elected into office.

3. If they do not vote in an election, then I feel that they don't have the right to speak their mind about the elected officials because they didn't vote for anybody.

4. What I mean by this is that they should never cheat, steal, kill, or damage anybody else's property.

5. If they break the laws, then they are setting an immoral example for future generations.

6. If we are good role models for future generations, then we can build a great country to live in.

7. This tax money, in theory, goes to the schools, police force, parks, etc.

8. I know it seems like paying taxes is a burden and unfair sometimes, but they do truly help our communities become a better place.

9. Since the above mentioned qualities are all supportive of making a better community, I feel that voting, being a law abiding citizen, and paying our required taxes show that we are good citizens.

10. We should all strive to be good citizens, and these three aspects are just simple ways we can be exactly that.

> **Q231. What are the most important qualities of a good teacher?**

A. Essay Outline

Argument: I think back to my best teacher and he had three specific qualities; he was always fair and consistent, he was never rude or condescending, and he was easy to approach.
Support 1: The first of the most important qualities a good teacher should have is being fair and consistent.
Support 2: The next most important quality of a good teacher is to never be rude or to be condescending.
Support 3: The final quality that I hold to be important of a good teacher is to be approachable.
Thesis: A teacher who is fair and impartial, who is not rude or condescending, and who is open and welcoming is a good teacher in my opinion.

B. Model Essay

We have hopefully all had a good teacher that we remember in our lives. Thinking back to the best teacher I have ever had, Mr. Hillshire possessed three specific qualities. He was always fair and consistent, he was never rude or condescending, and he was easy to approach. Because he had all of these qualities, I saw him as a good teacher, and so did all of the other students.

The first of the most important qualities a good teacher should have is being fair and consistent. Mr. Hillshire never had favorites and he held all the students to the same level of discipline and love. If you were an A+ student, but forgot your homework, you got the same punishment as the C student. This might seem unfair, but in actuality, it is very fair. It showed me that he kept to his rules consistently in the classroom, which made it very easy to know what his expectations of you were.

The next most important quality of a good teacher is to never be rude or to be condescending. Teachers who make us cry, or make us feel bad about ourselves are not good teachers in my eyes. If I did something wrong in class, Mr. Hillshire corrected me on it, but he didn't do it in a way where it lessened my desire to learn and to make mistakes. Students often make mistakes because it is a part of the learning process. But, if a teacher harshly criticized me or embarrassed me in front of the other students, I would not be as willing to answer a question in the future.

The final quality that I hold to be important of a good teacher is to be approachable. If students find the teacher to be unapproachable, they will not be able to ask for help if they are confused on a specific topic or skill that was discussed in the class. Mr. Hillshire was not best friends with the students, but rather, he granted an open and welcoming opportunity for the less confident students, like me, to ask for clarification in the classroom. There is a very careful balance between being too friendly and being approachable.

A teacher who is fair and impartial, who is not rude or condescending, and who is open and welcoming is a good teacher in my opinion. Possessing these qualities affords all students an equal chance to excel in the classroom, not just the ones who are considered to be the teacher's pets or favorites. I will never forget Mr. Hillshire because he had all of these qualities.

C. Useful Expressions

1. Thinking back to the best teacher I have ever had, Mr. Hillshire possessed three specific qualities.

2. He was always fair and consistent, he was never rude or condescending, and he was easy to approach.

3. This might seem unfair, but in actuality, it is very fair.

4. It showed me that he kept to his rules consistently in the classroom, which made it very easy to know what his expectations of you were.

5. He was always fair and consistent, he was never rude or condescending, and he was easy to approach.

6. This might seem unfair, but in actuality, it is very fair.

7. It showed me that he kept to his rules consistently in the classroom, which made it very easy to know what his expectations of you were.

8. Mr. Hillshire was not best friends with the students, but rather, he granted an open and welcoming opportunity for the less confident students, like me, to ask for clarification in the classroom.

9. There is a very careful balance between being too friendly and being approachable.

10. Possessing these qualities affords all students an equal chance to excel in the classroom, not just the ones who are considered to be the teacher's pets or favorites.

Q232. What qualities does a good student have to have?

A. Essay Outline

Argument: Being a good student means always being prepared, managing time well, and asking for help when it's needed.
Support 1: One of the most essential qualities a student should possess is to be hard working and motivated.
Support 2: The next important quality of a good student is to have a good sense of time management.
Support 3: Finally, not being timid in the classroom is a great quality of a good student.
Thesis: Having these three qualities will benefit a student academically.

B. Model Essay

Often times, we are under great pressure by our parents, teachers, and peers to be a good student. But what does being a good student mean? It means being a hard worker and having the motivation to finish all the assigned tasks properly. It means managing your time well. It also means not being afraid to ask for help if you don't understand something. Having possessed all of these skills made me a very successful student in school.

One of the most essential qualities a student should possess is to be hard working and motivated. What exactly does hard working and motivated mean? It means that the student should always do their homework, and they should pay attention in the classroom to the instructor. A good student will successfully complete all of their assigned tasks, and they will do it by putting their best effort forward. Also, they will not have to be told to study on their own; they will be intrinsically motivated to study themselves.

The next important quality of a good student is that they have a good sense of time management. Schools require a lot of time to accomplish their assignments, so a student needs to be able to properly manage the time that it will take to finish these assigned tasks. They will know how far out they should start preparing for their ten-page essay assignment, and they will also know how much time they need to study for the big final exams next week. They will not be a procrastinator and wait until the last minute to start their assignments.

Finally, not being timid in the classroom is a great quality of a good student. If you are timid in the classroom, then you will not be willing to ask for clarification when you don't understand something the teacher says, leaving you lost and confused. I'm not saying that the student needs to ask a lot of questions to be a good student. I'm only stating that if they are unsure of something or confused about a specific topic, they should be unafraid to ask the teacher for more of an explanation.

In school, students should have many qualities to be academically successful. These three qualities are that they should be hard working and motivated, have a good sense of time management, and not be timid about asking for clarification. Having these three qualities will benefit a student academically, as they did for me.

C. Useful Expressions

1. Often times, we are under great pressure by our parents, teachers, and peers to be a good student.

2. Having possessed all of these skills made me a very successful student in school.

3. One of the most essential qualities a student should possess is to be hard working and motivated.

4. A good student will successfully complete all of their assigned tasks, and they will do it by putting their best effort forward.

5. They will know how far out they should start preparing for their ten-page essay assignment, and they will also know how much time they need to study for the big final exams next week.

6. They will not be a procrastinator and wait until the last minute to start their assignments.

7. I'm not saying that the student needs to ask a lot of questions to be a good student.

8. I'm only stating that if they are unsure of something or confused about a specific topic, they should be unafraid to ask the teacher for more of an explanation.

9. Having these three qualities will benefit a student academically, as they did for me.

> **Q233. What would you change about your country if you were given the opportunity?**

A. Essay Outline

Argument: I would love to see three things change in the U.S.A.: more diversity and acceptance in all parts of the country, less arguing between politicians, and no reporting of negative news.
Support 1: The first thing I would change is to have more diversity and acceptance in all parts of the country.
Support 2: The second item that I would love to see changed in the USA is for there to be less arguing between the politicians, including the disputes received by the public.
Support 3: The last item I would make amendments to in America is the media's reporting of negative news.
Thesis: To conclude, if Americans could see more diversity and acceptance, more civil political settings, and more positive media influences, then the "Land of the Free and the Home of the Brave" would be an even better country to live in.

B. Model Essay

To many Americans, the United States of America is a great country with very few problems. To others, the country has many flaws that they would fix. I fall in between these two opinions. I love America and feel very fortunate to have been born there, but I would love to see three things change in the U.S.A.: more diversity and acceptance in all parts of the country, less arguing between politicians, and no reporting of negative news.

The first thing I would change is to have more diversity and acceptance in all parts of the country. America has come a long way since the Civil Rights Act and the Emancipation Proclamation, but it has a lot more it can grow. America is viewed as an equal opportunity country by many, yet there are still many racist and prejudiced people, whether it is against race, gender, nationality, or religion. The great thing about America is that you are supposed to have the freedom to possess your own beliefs, just as long as they don't break the constitutional rules, such as killing other humans.

The second item that I would love to see changed in the USA is for there to be less arguing between the politicians, including the disputes received by the public. I would encourage the politicians to bridge the gap between the right-wing (Conservative) and the left-wing (Democrat) politicians. Making a defined three-party system might help to alleviate some of these tensions between the current two-party system. If we can take away the constant battles and political back-lashings, then maybe, just maybe, our country might be able to move forward, instead of backward, like its current track.

The last item I would make amendments to in America is the media's reporting of negative news. Too often, the media only reports deaths, shootings, and other negative things. But, wouldn't it be nice if we could see a story about people helping each other, instead of hurting each other? Having positive role-models and media would greatly affect our country. Imagine how much respectable actions would be done, if we saw other's good actions being reported. They too would want to be rewarded for their positive contributions in life, rather than the 'bad' people in the country being glorified by the news.

To conclude, if Americans could see more diversity and acceptance, more civil political settings, and more positive media influences, then the "Land of the Free and the Home of the Brave" would be an even better country to live in. Americans have it so good, compared to other countries in the world, yet Americans want more. How about we, as Americans be thankful for all that we have and learn to make what we have been given an even better place to live?

C. Useful Expressions

1. To many Americans, the United States of America is a great country with very few problems. To others, the country has many flaws that they would fix. I fall in between these two opinions.

2. I love America and feel very fortunate to have been born there, but I would love to see three things change in the U.S.A.

3. America has come a long way since the Civil Rights Act and the Emancipation Proclamation, but it has a lot more it can grow.

4. The great thing about America is that you are supposed to have the freedom to possess your own beliefs, just as long as they don't break the constitutional rules, such as killing other humans.

5. I would encourage the politicians to bridge the gap between the right-wing (Conservative) and the left-wing (Democrat) politicians.

6. Making a defined three-party system might help to alleviate some of these tensions between the current two-party system.

7. But, wouldn't it be nice if we could see a story about people helping each other, instead of hurting each other?

8. Having positive role-models and media would greatly affect our country.

9. Americans have it so good, compared to other countries in the world, yet Americans want more.

10. How about we, as Americans be thankful for all that we have and learn to make what we have been given an even better place to live?

Q234. Do you agree or disagree with the following statement? An eye for an eye. Why or why not?

A. Essay Outline

Argument: Despite my human instincts to react negatively back toward others, I do not agree with this statement.
Support 1: To begin, there are other options to resolve this conflict.
Support 2: Next, you should be the better person in this situation.
Support 3: Lastly, hitting them will only cause further harm to you in the future.
Thesis: Since retaliating back only causes more harm than good, I do not agree with the statement of "an eye for an eye."

B. Model Essay

The saying "An eye for an eye" means that if someone does something negative to you, you should do something negative back to them. Despite my human instincts to react negatively back toward others, I do not agree with this statement. There are other options to resolve conflicts, you should be the better person and not resort to their childish actions, and they are not worth the negative backlash you'd receive for doing wrong to them. I will use one specific example to demonstrate my reasoning: somebody physically harming you by hitting you.

To begin, there are other options to resolve this conflict. When somebody hits you, your first instinct is to want to hit them back. However, this is not the best option. The best option is to avoid them in the future and to cut off all contact with them. This type of person is not somebody you want or need in your life. Another approach would be to talk to them about their rude, violent, childish act of resorting to physical violence for their own anger problems. One more final option is to leave them a note expressing your feelings about their physical assault. However, I find notes to be an elementary-aged thing to do. So, I do not recommend this option.

Next, you should be the better person in this situation. If you follow the eye-for-an-eye rule in life, then you are just as negative of a person as they are. Just because somebody hits you, or steals from you, or even spreads negative rumors about you, it doesn't mean you should stoop down to their level by doing the same immature acts. As early as elementary school, we can control our feelings and choose who we want to surround ourselves by. So this means that we do not need to be around those that are negative or bring us down. So, instead of being on their destructive level, we can choose to avoid them and be the better person in the situation.

Lastly, hitting them will only cause further harm to you in the future. If you resort to physically harming them back, it will only prove that you are a violent person too. This then will get you in trouble at school, at your job, with your friends, or with your family. It will most likely make you look bad to those that care about you, and in return, you might lose people you care about because of your rash decision making skills.

In conclusion, I do not agree with the statement of "an eye for an eye." Retaliating towards those that do negatives to you is of no benefit to you in your future. You should be the better person, try to resolve the conflict through another means, and learn from the mistakes that got you in that position in the first place. If you live by these simple rules, you will have a happy life without resorting to revenge upon others that will only fill your heart with hate and pain.

C. Useful Expressions

1. There are other options to resolve conflicts, you should be the better person and not resort to their childish actions, and they are not worth the negative backlash you'd receive for doing wrong to them.

2. I will use one specific example to demonstrate my reasoning: somebody physically harming you by hitting you.

3. When somebody hits you, your first instinct is to want to hit them back.

4. Another approach would be to talk to them about their rude, violent, childish act of resorting to physical violence for their own anger problems.

5. Just because somebody hits you, or steals from you, or even spreads negative rumors about you, it doesn't mean you should stoop down to their level by doing the same immature acts.

6. As early as elementary school, we can control our feelings and choose who we want to surround ourselves by.

7. This then will get you in trouble at school, at your job, with your friends, or with your family.

8. It will most likely make you look bad to those that care about you, and in return, you might lose people you care about because of your rash decision making skills.

9. Retaliating towards those that do negatives to you is of no benefit to you in your future.

10. If you live by these simple rules, you will have a happy life without resorting to revenge upon others that will only fill your heart with hate and pain.

> **Q235. What is the most important job or task you have ever had? Why was it important?**

A. Essay Outline

Argument: The most important task that I was assigned was being the Barracks NCO (Non-commissioned Officer) for one and half years in Daegu, South Korea.
Support 1: I had to keep everything well-organized.
Support 2: Second, people relied on me to do my job properly.
Support 3: Third, I had to conduct presentations to the top officials of the US Army in the Daegu area.
Thesis: Since it taught me valuable lessons of organization, people skills, and presenting in front of high-ranking officials, being the Barracks NCO was my most important task or job that I was given.

B. Model Essay

    Some important tasks or jobs that I have had were being a manager of a food stand at an amusement park, teaching Sunday school to Kindergarten-aged children for 10 years, and assisting in raising another woman's baby for two years as a nanny. These jobs were all important for various reasons, but the most important task that I was assigned was being the Barracks NCO (Non-commissioned Officer) for one and half years in Daegu, South Korea. Barracks are military housing for soldiers who live with one other roommate on the military base, and an NCO is a leader in the US Army who is responsible to various tasks.

    First of all, the reason that my job was important was that I had to keep everything well-organized. My job entailed the issuing out of keys and storage lockers, the assignment of roommates and cleaning duties, and the rotating of mattresses. It also involved keeping a painstakingly precise inventory of all the furniture items in the four-story building. Because of my organization skills, the almost 180 residents had bug-free rooms, well-maintained furniture, as well as a safe room to stay in due to the strict key control regulations.

    Second, people relied on me to do my job properly. My job was not just about me, but about taking care of others. So, if one of my tasks slipped through the cracks, it would send a harmful ripple-effect to all of the incoming soldiers who were brand new to Korea. I had to always make sure that everything ran smoothly, and that I was never off my game when it came to running the soldiers' dorm-like housing. If I forgot to collect a key from a soldier before they left the country, the current resident soldier would have to share one key with their incoming soldier roommate. This would cause a lot of stress to the newbie, which was not helpful to the already unfamiliar surroundings.

    Third, I had to conduct presentations to the top officials of the US Army in the Daegu area. These were the leaders of the Army bases who were much higher than me in the promotion scale. I had a lot of pressure to ensure that I had accurate rosters of all incoming personnel and out-going personnel, the appropriate work-order requests (repair of furniture) from the soldiers documented, and a wide variety of other information on colorful spreadsheets. I remember one time when my boss, known as a First Sergeant, was asked a difficult question, and he was unsure of the answer, but I stepped in as a lower ranking soldier and saved him. This made my First Sergeant relieved, because he knew he could rely on my for all the difficult situations that were presented to me.

    Running a building of over a hundred and seventy soldiers was not an easy task. I was a little nervous about taking on such a large project, but I knew it was an important job that needed to be done. So, I took on the important challenge of successfully maintaining the organization of the soldier dormitories. It taught me valuable lessons of organization, people skills, and presenting in-front of high-ranking officials. So, this is why it was my most important task or job that I was given.

C. Useful Expressions

1. Some important tasks or jobs that I have had were being a manager of a food stand at an amusement park, teaching Sunday school to Kindergarten-aged children for 10 years, and assisting in raising another woman's baby for two years as a nanny.

2. Barracks are military housing for soldiers who live with one other roommate on the military base, and an NCO is a leader in the US Army who is responsible to various tasks.

3. My job entailed the issuing out of keys and storage lockers, the assignment of roommates and cleaning duties, and the rotating of mattresses.

4. It also involved keeping a painstakingly precise inventory of all the furniture items in the four-story building.

5. Second, people relied on me to do my job properly.

6. So, if one of my tasks slipped through the cracks, it would send a harmful ripple-effect to all of the incoming soldiers who were brand new to Korea.

7. I had to always make sure that everything ran smoothly, and that I was never off my game when it came to running the soldiers' dorm-like housing.

8. I had a lot of pressure to ensure that I had accurate rosters of all incoming personnel and out-going personnel, the appropriate work-order requests (repair of furniture) from the soldiers documented, and a wide variety of other information on colorful spreadsheets.

9. I remember one time when my boss, known as a First Sergeant, was asked a difficult question, and he was unsure of the answer, but I stepped in as a lower ranking soldier and saved him.

10. Running a building of over a hundred and seventy soldiers was not an easy task.

Q236. What are the advantages and disadvantages of studying abroad?

A. Essay Outline

Argument: Studying abroad has both many advantages and disadvantages of studying abroad that range from financial burdens, to excelling in a new language.
Support 1: Some disadvantages of studying abroad are that the parents might become overwhelmed financially, and the students will get frustrated by the language barrier.
Support 2: Some advantages of studying abroad are that the student will develop a more open mind, their language skills will improve, and they can earn credits towards their college degree.
Support 3: I would have loved to been given the opportunity to have traveled abroad so that I could have made more friends from all around the world.
Thesis: To summarize, studying abroad has some highly desirable aspects, but it also has some less desirable aspects.

B. Model Essay

Studying abroad has always been a popular desire for students wishing to learn a new culture and to improve upon their language skills of their destination's mother-tongue. There are both many advantages and disadvantages of studying abroad. These range from financial burdens to excelling in a new language.

Let me begin with discussing the disadvantages of studying abroad. First, the parents will be overwhelmed with a large financial burden. Traveling is not cheap, and on top of that, the cost of living can be outrageous in the foreign country. In addition, the student might become more frustrated with themselves. This is partly due to their lack of language skills or maybe the extreme cultural differences.

On the contrary, there are numerous advantages. The foreign-bound student will develop a more open-mind to other cultures, all while they are able to experience traveling around the world. Also, the student will create a higher level of independence and will have many opportunities to improve their language skills. Often times, college credits can be earned towards their degree at some universities.

I was never given the amazing chance to travel abroad during my school years. So even though I would miss my family and friends during the holidays, I would love to been given the opportunity to travel abroad and to study. On top of the many advantages listed above, I could make new friends and business contacts for future jobs. Networking is a vital tool when it comes to competing in the job-market of today. Who knows, one of the people I meet through my travels could be my open door into obtaining my dream job!

To summarize, studying abroad has some highly desirable aspects, but it also has some less desirable aspects. It is a difficult predicament to be in, but the positives far outweigh the negatives when it comes to this specific situation. A lifetime of knowledge while being fully immersed in a language is far more beneficial to me in my future than the possibility of missing my family for a short period of time.

C. Useful Expressions

1. Studying abroad has always been a popular desire for students wishing to learn a new culture and to improve upon their language skills of their destination's mother-tongue.

2. There are both many advantages and disadvantages of studying abroad. These range from financial burdens, to excelling in a new language.

3. Let me begin with discussing the disadvantages of studying abroad.

4. This is partly due to their lack of language skills or maybe the extreme cultural differences.

5. The foreign-bound student will develop a more open-mind to other cultures, all while they are able to experience traveling around the world.

6. Often times, college credits can be earned towards their degree at some universities.

7. So even though I would miss my family and friends during the holidays, I would love to been given the opportunity to travel abroad and to study.

8. Networking is a vital tool when it comes to competing in the job-market of today.

9. To summarize, studying abroad has some highly desirable aspects, but it also has some less desirable aspects.

10. It is a difficult predicament to be in, but the positives far outweigh the negatives when it comes to this specific situation.

> **Q237. Describe your dream job. Why is it your dream job?**

A. Essay Outline

Argument: My dream job is work at an all English immersion program for infants through Kindergarten.
Support 1: To begin with, I have been teaching for 17 years now.
Support 2: Furthermore, I truly enjoy the rewards I receive from the light-bulbs clicking on in young learners.
Support 3: Finally, it has been scientifically proven that learning a new language at a young age is easier for the 'student,' so I want to help encourage this behavior for the future native English speakers.
Thesis: As you can see, I have the experience, the knowledge, and the passion for teaching young children, which is why working in an all English immersion program for young children is my dream job.

B. Model Essay

    I love my current job of being an elementary/middle school/high school/university-aged English Language teacher, but it is not my dream job. My dream job still entails working with children, but just in a different environment. I would love to work at an all English emersion program for infants through Kindergarten. First, it is what I am best at and have more experience in. Second, I can enjoy the rewards of the environment. Third, it is the most appropriate age level to expose children to learning a new language.

    To begin with, I have been teaching for 17 years now. I started assisting my step-mother when I was 13 years old in her Sunday school classes and fell in love with teaching. Through this experience, I was able to grow and learn as a teacher and to learn my preferences. I graduated from my university with a teaching degree in early childhood and elementary education; however, my specialty was in the early childhood portion. I excelled in all of my classes and received top marks for my experience and knowledge of the younger children's mentalities. So, working in a younger learners' environment is definitely my dream job.

    Furthermore, I truly enjoy the rewards I receive from the light-bulbs clicking on in their young minds. In teaching, we call it the 'a-ha' moment. It's the moment when somebody finally understands something, or they finally use something properly. I'll never forget an 'a-ha' moment I experienced in my current school with a Kindergarten-aged child. Throughout the past few months, she always had a candy, and she always wanted her candy to be opened. So, I kept reinforcing the words, "Open my candy, please." Well, one day, I was downstairs in the lobby waiting for someone, and this little girl was with her mom. She had a piece of candy in her hand as usual, and the long awaited moment happened! She said in a sweet and confident voice using English, to her Korean mother, "Open my candy, please." I was so shocked and excited at the same time. These are the moments that teachers live for, that reward us, and that show us our students do listen to us!

    Finally, it has been scientifically proven that learning a new language at a young age is easier for the 'student'. I struggle in learning a new language because I am constantly trying to translate the unfamiliar language into my own familiar language. This takes time, brain power, and causes a great deal of frustration to me. On the other hand, an infant through Kindergarten-aged child doesn't translate words. Rather, they learn the context of a word and use it in a trial and error process, until they realize the pattern the word should be used in. For example, young children learn the word 'cat' and then they see a dog. They call the dog a 'cat' because they don't know any better. That is until somebody corrects them. Now, all four legged animals are cats and dogs to them. They continue this pattern throughout their early life learning new words and making mistakes. So, I want to help encourage this behavior for the future native English speakers.

As you can see, I have the experience, the knowledge, and the passion for teaching young children. Through my numerous years of experience in educating the youth, I hope that one day in the future, I will be able to work in a full immersion English as a Second Language program. I am very happy with my current job, but I hope that in 20 years or so, I can achieve my dream job.

C. Useful Expressions

1. First, it is what I am best at and have more experience in.

2. Second, I can enjoy the rewards of the environment.

3. Through this experience, I was able to grow and learn as a teacher and to learn my preferences.

4. So, working in a younger learners' environment is definitely my dream job.

5. It's the moment when somebody finally understands something, or they finally use something properly.

6. I'll never forget an 'a-ha' moment I experienced in my current school with a Kindergarten-aged child.

7. Finally, it has been scientifically proven that learning a new language at a young age is easier for the 'student'.

8. On the other hand, an infant through Kindergarten- aged child doesn't translate words. Rather, they learn the context of a word and use it in a trial and error process, until they realize the pattern the word should be used in.

9. So, I want to help encourage this behavior for the future native English speakers.

10. Through my numerous years of experience in educating the youth, I hope that one day in the future, I will be able to work in a full immersion English as a Second Language program.

Q238. At what age is it appropriate to allow a child to stay at home alone?

A. Essay Outline

Argument: I will state that a child, who is responsible and has some other variables included, can be left home alone at the age of ten.
Support 1: The first reason is based on the child's personality.
Support 2: This leads me into my next point that it depends on why the child needs to be left alone in the first place.
Support 3: Lastly, the length of time affects the age that is appropriate for a child to be alone in their home.
Thesis: To sum up my thoughts, a child at the age of ten can be left unattended, but only meeting certain conditions.

B. Model Essay

This is a very challenging question; at what age is it appropriate to allow a child to stay at home alone? I strongly believe that it depends on the child's personality, the reason the child needs to be left alone, and the length of time the child is left unattended. No one child is the exact same as another, so to give an exact age is not accurate. So, I will state that a child, who is responsible and has some other variables included, can be left home alone at the age of ten.

As stated above, there are a variety of factors that determine whether a child can be left home alone or not. The first reason is based on the child's personality. In my case, I was left home alone as early as eight years old. My mother felt that I was independent enough to take care of myself and responsible enough to do what was right. I was able to cook microwaveable meals, brush my teeth and get ready for bed, all on my own.

This leads me into my next point that it depends on why the child needs to be left alone in the first place. Again, in my situation, my mother had to work, and she couldn't afford to pay for a babysitter. Sometimes, circumstances arise that make it difficult to provide for your children successfully, but my mother did the best she could. She did ask a neighbor to keep an eye on me from her house, by just observing me and calling me once and a while. So, I was not completely unattended.

Lastly, the length of time affects the age that is appropriate for a child to be alone in their home. At the age of ten, a child can be left alone for a few hours and should not have any major catastrophes occur, just as long as strict guidelines are observed. A ten year old child should not be left alone for more than five hours though, because they might have difficulty preparing their meals or going to bed on time.

To sum up my thoughts, a child at the age of ten can be left unattended, but only after following the suggestions listed above. They should have set rules to follow, contact numbers to call, and somebody to observe them from a distance. By being left alone at a younger age, children learn a great deal of independent skills that will be vital to them in their adult lives.

C. Useful Expressions

1. I strongly believe that it depends on the child's personality, the reason the child needs to be left alone, and the length of time the child is left unattended.

2. Not one child is the exact same as another, so to give an exact age is not accurate.

3. So, I will state that a child, who is responsible and has some other variables included, can be left home alone at the age of ten.

4. As stated above, there are a variety of factors that determine whether a child can be left home alone or not.

5. The first reason is based on the child's personality.

6. This leads me into my next point that it depends on why the child needs to be left alone in the first place.

7. Again, in my situation, my mother had to work, and she couldn't afford to pay for a babysitter.

8. Lastly, the length of time affects the age that is appropriate for a child to be alone in their home.

9. At the age of ten, a child can be left alone for a few hours and should not have any major catastrophes occur, just as long as strict guidelines are observed.

10. To sum up my thoughts, a child at the age of ten can be left unattended, but only after following the suggestions listed above.

> **Q239. Some people say that the quality of a product is more important. Others say that the price of a product is more important. Which statement do you agree with and why?**

A. Essay Outline

Argument: I believe quality is more important than its price tag.
Support 1: For starters, cheap prices usually mean a cheap quality product.
Support 2: Next, I can have trust in the product that it will work properly.
Support 3: To conclude, if my product did break down, I have a guaranteed warranty with higher quality products.
Thesis: Since money is of no importance when it comes to the functioning capabilities of a product, I prefer quality over price.

B. Model Essay

Imagine you are in the market to buy a computer. You have the choice between a high quality laptop, and a less pricy computer. Which would you choose? I without a doubt would buy the higher quality laptop for the following three reasons: cheap prices usually mean cheap quality, trust in the product to work properly, and guaranteed warranty.

For starters, cheap prices usually mean a cheap quality product. In the case of the laptop, a cheap computer doesn't come with some of the desired programs. I just bought a laptop myself, and the cheaper computers did not have the programs I wanted. So I went for a more expensive product that had higher quality.

Next, I can have trust in the product that it will work properly. When it comes to quality versus price, the price doesn't matter when it comes to my product functioning properly. In the example of the laptop, if I bought a cheap computer, it would most likely break down in a few short months. The cheaper products are generally made from cheaper quality products. Therefore, cheap prices mean a lower quality computer.

To conclude, if my product did break down, I have a guaranteed warranty with higher quality products. Most high quality products are produced by a name-brand. Because of this, they almost always come with a warranty on their products. Mistakes can happen, and something might happen to my computer, so I want to be ensured that my money spent on something is not wasted.

Since money is of no importance when it comes to the functioning capabilities of a product, I prefer quality over price. I don't want to lose out on my money due to faulty materials used in the production of a cheap product. To me, my time in fixing a broken cheap product is more of a hassle and frustration than buying a more expensive product that I know will work.

C. Useful Expressions

1. Imagine you are in the market to buy a computer. You have the choice between a high quality laptop and a less pricy computer. Which would you choose?

2. I without a doubt would buy the higher quality laptop for the following three reasons: cheap prices usually mean cheap quality, trust in the product to work properly, and guaranteed warranty.

3. For starters, cheap prices usually mean a cheap quality product.

4. In the case of the laptop, a cheap computer doesn't come with some of the desired programs.

5. When it comes to quality versus price, the price doesn't matter when it comes to my product functioning properly.

6. In the example of the laptop, if I bought a cheap computer, it would most likely break down in a few short months.

7. Because of this, they almost always come with a warranty on their products.

8. Mistakes can happen, and something might happen to my computer, so I want to be ensured that my money spent on something is not wasted.

9. Since money is of no importance when it comes to the functioning capabilities of a product, I prefer quality over price.

10. I don't want to lose out on my money due to faulty materials used in the production of a cheap product.

> **Q240. How will you help a foreigner learn about your country?**

A. Essay Outline

Argument: I feel that the best way to help a foreigner learn about America is through three things: sightseeing, movies and music, and socializing with my friends and family.
Support 1: The first way I can help a foreigner learn about my country is my taking them around the various tourist spots in America.
Support 2: Secondly, I can introduce them to American movies and music.
Support 3: Finally, socializing with my friends and family will be the best way for the out-of-towner to see my culture.
Thesis: Since using a variety of tactics will be the best options for a foreigner to learn about my country, I would show them tourist spots, movies and music, and my friends' and family's lifestyles.

B. Model Essay

There are so many ways to assist a foreigner in learning about my country. America has a large variety of places to see and things to do. I feel that the best way to help a foreigner learn about America is through three things: sightseeing, movies and music, and socializing with my friends and family.

The first way I can help a foreigner learn about my country is my taking them around the various tourist spots in America. Through these different locations, the foreigner will be able to learn the history and culture of my country. For instance, if I take a foreigner to New York City, I would show them the Statue of Liberty. By doing this, they can see how many people have come to America from other countries.

Secondly, I can introduce them to American movies and music. I feel that music and movies show a skewed version of our culture, but it will still be an entertaining experience for them. Movies, such as American Beauty, and Precious show a more realistic side of the American society. If we can expose the foreigner to just a taste of the American music and movies, then they can better understand our differences and similarities to their own cultures.

Finally, socializing with my friends and family will be the best way for the out-of-towner to see my culture. When I was in a new country, South Korea, hanging out with native people from that country helped me greatly to learn about the Korean culture. If I had solely relied on movies and music or books, I would have not learned as much of the little nuances of this conservative, yet complex culture. One example was that I gained knowledge about the things that are taboo in the Korean society.

Since using a variety of tactics will be the best options for a foreigner to learn about my country, I would show them tourist spots, movies and music, and my friends' and family's lifestyles. By doing a mixture of all of these things, a person who is unfamiliar with the American culture will gain a better view of how people from the USA live, work, and play.

C. Useful Expressions

1. There are so many ways to assist a foreigner in learning about my country.

2. I feel that the best way to help a foreigner learn about America is through three things: sightseeing, movies and music, and socializing with my friends and family.

3. Through these different locations, the foreigner will be able to learn the history and culture of my country.

4. For instance, if I take a foreigner to New York City, I would show them the Statue of Liberty.

5. I feel that music and movies show a skewed version of our culture, but it will still be an entertaining experience for them.

6. If we can expose the foreigner to just a taste of the American music and movies, then they can better understand our differences and similarities to their own cultures.

7. Finally, socializing with my friends and family will be the best way for the out-of-towner to see my culture.

8. If I had solely relied on movies and music or books, I would have not learned as much of the little nuances of this conservative, yet complex culture.

9. Since using a variety of tactics will be the best options for a foreigner to learn about my country, I would show them tourist spots, movies and music, and my friends' and family's lifestyles.

10. By doing a mixture of all of these things, a person who is unfamiliar with the American culture will gain a better view of how people from the USA live, work, and play.

ABOUT THE EDITOR

LIKE TEST PREP

LIKE TEST PREP Series

Advanced Reading, Writing, and Grammar for Test Prep

1. Teaches you how to do better on reading and writing tests
2. Tips based on reading, writing, and grammar research
3. Vocabulary, Sample Questions, and Question Type Analysis

60 Model Essays

60 Challenging Essay Questions and Sample Essays

120 Writing Topics with Sample Essays

120 Essay Questions and Sample Essays

120 Speaking Topics with Sample Answers

120 Speaking Questions and Sample Answers

240 Writing Topics with Sample Essays

240 Essay Questions and Sample Essays

240 Speaking Topics with Sample Answers

240 Speaking Questions and Sample Answers

120 Writing Summaries

120 Reading/Listening Summary Questions

120 Sample Summaries

Meet Amazing Americans Workbook Series

Meet Amazing Americans Workbook

Free mp3 at www.liketestprep.com

CPSIA information can be obtained
at www.ICGtesting.com
Printed in the USA
LVHW061155120120
643351LV00019B/1888/P